D1221790

Radhakrishnan
and the Ways
of Oneness
of East *and* West

Radhakrishnan
and the Ways
of Oneness *of* East
and West

Troy Wilson Organ

OHIO UNIVERSITY PRESS  ATHENS

LUTHER NORTHWESTERN
SEMINARY LIBRARY
2375 Como Avenue
St. Paul, MN 55108

B5134
.R34 O7

© Copyright 1989 by Troy Wilson Organ
Printed in the United States of America
All rights reserved

Organ, Troy Wilson.
    Radhakrishnan and the ways of oneness of East and West / Troy
Wilson Organ.
        p.   cm.
    Bibliography: p.
    ISBN 0-8214-0936-0 (alk. paper)
    1. Radhakrishnan, S. (Sarvepalli), 1888-1975. 2. Philosophy,
Comparative. 3. East and West. I. Title.
B5.134.R334074   1989
181'.4—dc20   89-9397
                                            CIP

Ohio University Press books are printed on acid-free paper. ∞

LUTHER NORTHWESTERN
SEMINARY LIBRARY
2375 Como Avenue
St. Paul, MN 55108

CONTENTS

Part One
Radhakrishnan:
The Man in His Writings

"*I*t is very difficult to write about Radhakrishnan without suffering qualms of a guilty conscience. This is because what he may have said or written is of little value compared to what he is."[1] So confesses P. J. Saher in his book *Eastern Wisdom and Western Thought*. But that is not how Radhakrishnan viewed his own life and writings. When Paul Arthur Schilpp, the editor of *The Philosophy of Sarvepalli Radhakrishnan*, vol. 8 in *The Library of Living Philosophers*, wrote to Radhakrishnan asking that he give more information about his personal life in the autobiographical section of the book, Radhakrishnan replied in a letter dated December 24, 1950, "I am not persuaded that the events of my life are of much interest to the readers of this volume. Besides, there is a sense in which our writings, though born out of ourselves, are worth more than what we are."[2] What one writes may be better than what one is! That may sometimes be the case. In another sense what one writes may be a good indicant of character and personality. This is the assumption I make in this study.

Radhakrishnan was a good man. I cite two examples. One occurred on March 17, 1955. He, as Vice-President of India, was asked to inaugurate a conference of the India Rifle Association. He began, "I am the last man to be called upon to inaugurate this Conference, for I have never in my life handled a rifle."[3] He closed his short speech with a gentle rebuke: "I do hope that these organizations will function without making men trigger-happy, military-minded, aggressive or violent in spirit."[4] Although such an admonition may seem naive, it bespeaks the kind of man he was. It calls to mind another statement of his: "Even as the democratic way forbids in internal problems, direct action, mob rule or resort to violence, in international problems also we have to assume the reasonableness of human beings and adopt methods of negotiation, discussion, adjustment and agreement."[5] The other example was his first act upon becoming President of India on May 11, 1962: he reduced his salary to a bare minimum.[6]

Radhakrishnan was a tireless worker for good causes. His personal courage, strength, and dedication can be expressed in a quotation from Stadtholder with which he closed his book *Kalki; or, the Future of Civilization*: "I have no need to hope in order to undertake; nor to succeed in order to persevere."[7] Schilpp wrote in the preface to the volume on Radhakrishnan, "Throughout the twelve years of the existence of this Library, no other philosopher has given of his time more unstintedly to this project than has Professor Radhakrishnan."[8]

Radhakrishnan opens his volume on the philosophy of Tagore with this quotation from Hegel: "The condemnation which a great man lays upon the world is to force it to explain him."[9] He applied the quotation to Tagore. Now it applies to Radhakrishnan. Part of the problem of trying to "explain" Radhakrishnan is that his active participation in the life of his nation and in world affairs was not consistent with many of his expressions about the nature of philosophy and religion. He wrote that the aim of philosophy is "one of elevating man above worldliness, or making him superior to circumstance, of liberating his spirit from the thralldom of material things."[10] In the essay "My Search for Truth," which has been described as his "only actual Autobiography,"[11] Radhakrishnan confesses, "I am not quite at home in the conventional social functions by which life's troubles are tempered to most of us. . . . While I am essentially shy and lonely, I pass for a social and sociable man."[12] He writes of his "love of loneliness,"[13] of "an inner life of solitude" in which he "loves to dwell,"[14] and of his "need for a silent hour."[15] He, in the role of physician to the west—a role he seemed to enjoy—advises, "The West, giddy with its conquest over matter, needs periods of rest and contemplation."[16] "Many of us are afraid of looking into ourselves," he observes in The Hindu View of Life.[17] "So we become social beings and get away from the realities of our life."[18] These anchoretic statements seem strange from the pen of a man who during his lifetime was Vice-Chancellor of two Indian universities, Chancellor of another, India's Ambassador to the USSR, India's Ambassador to UNESCO, Chairman of the government university commission which set up university education in India, Vice-President of India for ten years, and President of India for five years.

There may be another way of explaining this side of Radhakrishnan's personality—the side which he calls his shyness. We must keep in mind that he was a Hindu—and a Brahmin. He wore a turban. But not for religious reasons. He admitted he wore it to give his remarks a halo of authority!

Radhakrishnan's Brahmanism comes out in The Hindu View of Life when he praises the caste system because it "does not favor the indiscriminate crossing of men and women."[19] He points out "the deplorable example of the Eurasians."[20] This is an expression of prejudice against a fine community in India. Some of India's outstanding people in high positions of leadership and scholarship in this century have been, and are, Anglo-Indians—or, if you prefer, Eurasians. Radhakrishnan's generalizations about the integration of Aryans and Dravidians is another strange blindness to social facts. A. R. Wadia writes "that after four thousand years Aryan and Dravids have not sufficiently mixed either in blood or in ideas to constitute one people."[21] Radhakrishnan's comments on Indian society do not reveal the awareness of problems and concern for their solution which one finds in the life and writings of Gandhi and Tagore. The result is, in the words of Wadia, "the orthodox [Hindus] look up to him as the champion of Hinduism, of which the caste system is regarded as the basic principle, whereas heterodox Hindus have been looking upon his philosophy as 'the Brahmin philosophy.'"[22]

I had only one contact with Radhakrishnan. That was at a tea in Delhi given in honor of Fulbrighters. I introduced myself as one who had been honored in being asked to write an essay in the volume celebrating his seventieth birthday. I soon gathered he preferred not to waste time conversing with a minor Western philosopher.

Radhakrishnan expresses what I call "his Brahmin attitude" in a small volume titled *True Knowledge*: "The true aim of education is not the acquisition of information, important though it may be, or acquisition of technical skills, though they are very essential to modern society. One must have that superior outlook, that outlook which goes beyond information and technical skill."[23] Radhakrishnan advises, "One must have the capacity to subsist in battle and to look at things, as they happen without any kind of inward disturbance or perturbation of one's being."[24] Now this may be called "Brahmanism" in India, but in the West I think it is known as "Stoic apathy." Perhaps "superior outlook" and the absence of "inward disturbance" were not the proper words. Serenity might have been what Radhakrishnan had in mind. In the volume *East and West in Religion* he says, "Only the man of serene mind can realize the spiritual meaning of life."[25] Swāmi Agehānanda Bhārati closes his article titled "Radhakrishnan and the Other Vedānta" in *The Philosophy of Sarvepalli Radhakrishnan* as follows: "There may be many pundits in India who know Sanskrit better and show more specific erudition than does Sir Sarvepalli, yet on the scale of world-wide contacts, which may yet give some hope in a mire of hopelessness, their weight must be less than that of the man who in our days holds out to the world the light of an ancient, serene, and sometimes mysteriously profound way of thinking and living."[26]

According to Radhakrishnan "there is a sense in which our writings . . . are worth more than what we are."[27] His two-volume work *Indian Philosophy* established him as a historian of philosophy; his *An Idealistic View of Life* evidenced that he was a creative metaphysician; and his *The Principle Upaniṣads, The Bhagavadgītā,* The *Dhammapada,* and *The Brahma* Sūtra removed all doubt as to his qualifications as a Sanskrit scholar.

I wish to confine more attention in this presentation to his less erudite writings. Many were prepared as lectures for lay audiences. Some are addresses given in administrative capacities. Others are articles written for publication in both popular and learned journals. All show him to be a master of style. V. S. Naravane has written, "There can be no doubt that Radhakrishnan's great influence in contemporary philosophical circles is partly the result of his eloquence. . . . In him we have a rare combination of style and scholarship."[28]

Many of his writings can be classified as essays, although essays are difficult to define. Samuel Johnson described the essay as "a loose sally of the mind, an irregular, undigested piece." J. B. Priestly solved the problem of definition: "An essay is the kind of composition written by an essayist." Many of Radhakrishnan's essays are like those of Emerson. They warm the heart, and sometimes challenge the mind. Bhārati says the philosophy of Radhakrishnan "inspires as it informs."[29] These are the writings which, as Radhakrishnan says, are "born of ourselves." They, therefore, mirror who he was.

I detect that Radhakrishnan enjoyed writing, that he was proud of his publications, and that he wanted to be remembered as an author. He reports that his early book *The Reign of Religion in Contemporary Philosophy*[30] had "a very warm reception,"[31] was praised beyond its merits,[32] had "many favorable reviews,"[33] and made the author "known as a writer on philosophy."[34] But not all agree with these evaluations. George P. Conger describes the book as Radhakrishnan's "intellectual measles and wild oats."[35] Most of Radhakrishnan's works, according to Conger, are calls to accept absolute idealism on the grounds of Radhakrishnan's own intuitions. He tends "to leap or plunge or swoon into the Absolute."[36] This, adds Conger, is "to go into spiritual reverse, and in one way or another to ignore or to relinquish the findings of the sciences and most of the fruits of Western culture."[37] Radhakrishnan is "vague," "indefinite," "inconsistent," "otherworldly," and "too Oriental to serve plenetary culture without further crystallization."[38] Conger concludes his evaluation by stating that Radhakrishnan melts into a monism two distinctions which the West will not give up: (1) the distinction between A and not-A, and (2) the distinction between the natural and the supranatural. An attack like this triggers a more reasonable and less emotional consideration of the writings of Radhakrishnan. I wish to do this by making five critical evaluations of the writings—and hence of the man: (1) His appeal to intuition; (2) His lack of consistency; (3) His neglect of analysis; (4) His use of platitudes; (5) His apologetic style.

1. His Appeal to Intuition.

Saher contends one will never understand Radhakrishnan until one recognizes that he was a mystic.[39] B. K. Mallik refers to him as a "Saint."[40]

Every Western philosopher knows that when conducting dialogue with an Indian philosopher who maintains linkage with traditional Hinduism that at some point the Indian will conclude with a quotation from an *Upaniṣad*—usually intoned in Sanskrit, or will announce "I feel that. . . ." Silence will then proclaim *quod erat demonstrandum*. Radhakrishnan was no exception. He in *An Idealist View of Life* recognizes three varieties of cognition: "sense experience, discursive reasoning, and intuitive apprehension."[41] Intuition, he contends, is self-validating. So intuition has priority over sharable experience and logical reasoning. But what is intuition? Robert W. Browning in a long and exhaustive analysis locates many different meanings of intuition in Radha-krishnan.[42] I discover fifteen in his article:

1. Sometimes it refers to processes.
2. Sometimes it refers to products.
3. Sometimes it refers to faculties, capacities, sources.
4. Sometimes it offers a fuller realization of what is known abstractly in symbols.
5. Sometimes it intimates what cannot be known in other ways.
6. Sometimes it refers to the dawning of a scientific generalization.
7. Sometimes it denotes knowledge of things in their concreteness.
8. Sometimes it refers to unitive knowledge of the One Reality.
9. Sometimes it accents the dynamism of thinking as against the results.
10. Sometimes it emphasizes spontaneous dynamism as opposed to mechanical movements.
11. Sometimes it denotes a mental capacity higher than discursive thought.
12. Sometimes it denotes a way to infallible knowledge.
13. Sometimes it denotes a way of knowing that should be carefully weighed.[43]
14. Sometimes it is said to be part of the self's fundamental nature, and sometimes it is said to be subject to cultivation.
15. Sometimes it is said to be a response of one's whole being to Reality rather than an epistemological term.

Browning attempts to bring order out of the plethora of uses of the concept by classifying Radhakrishnan's fifteen—or more—uses to five types:

1. Sensory intuition, that is, unanalyzed sensations.
2. Rational intuition, that is, direct understanding.
3. Ontological intuition,[44] that is, "Descrying of complex structure of fact and possible fact."[45]
4. Valuational intuition, that is, values in morals, art, and religion.
5. Integral experience, for example, the *tat tvam asi* experience.

Browning's analysis is a serious indictment of Radha-krishnan's claim to be a philosopher. A philosopher must use language carefully and exactly. An essayist uses language ingeniously and rhetorically. Browning kindly observes, "The broadness of Radhakrishnan's sweeps seems to leave certain vagueness or ambiguities."[46] Browning suggests that the urgency of Radhakrishnan's message may account for his ambiguities: "A prophet wishes to get the burden of his message across, and is not likely to commit the value distortions of pausing to settle everything everywhere with all the niceties which pro-perly titillate the intellectual sensualities of the respective breeds of us sedentary 'ruminant' philosophers."[47] Radha-krishnan can be forgiven, since he is a "prophet" rather than a philosopher!

I do not deny that Radhakrishnan had prophetic mo-ments, but I insist that he was a philosopher, although he was a philosopher on his own terms. He wrote, "Philoso-phy is not so much a conceptual reconstruction as an ex-hibition of insights."[48] For him a philosopher is not "an in-tellectual metaphysician paying homage to the logical in-tellect," but "an intuitive seer."[49] He rejected the view that philosophy deals with abstractions while poetry deals with life.[50]

In all considerations of comparative philosophy we must keep in mind that the terms *philosophy* and *philos-opher* have a wide range of denotations, for example, from Saint Augustine to Bertrand Russell; of designa-tions, for example, from scholasticism to logical positiv-ism; and of connotations, for example, from profound truthfulness to inconsequential quibble. Radhakrishnan in "Fragments of a Confession" almost casually states that his conception of the role of philosophy is very similar to that of Karl Marx; that is, philosophy should change life rather than merely interpret thought.[51] His close friend, B. K. Mallik, said Radhakrishnan's one aim was "to make the world free of the virus of conflict and hatred by the establishment of peace."[52]

Radhakrishnan was a pragmatist in the broad sense.

Philosophy as "mere knowledge," he says, is "of the nature of a decoration, an exhibit with no roots"[53] Philosophy should help us "not then so much think reality as live it . . . not so much know it as become it."[54] Saher refers to Aldous Huxley's message as "The Pursuit of Wisdom as the Goal of Life" and to Radhakrishnan's message as "The Application of Vedāntic Wisdom to Practical Life."[55] Radhakrishnan wished to change the lives of people. Mokṣa (freedom or liberation) was for him the telos of philosophy. At the close of his "Reply to Critics" he writes, "The common people of the world have never known freedom. The forces of privilege and oppression have kept the freedom for themselves, and the masses of people have had to work on conditions laid down for them or starve and die. . . . We must regain health, physical and spiritual. With this in mind let us proclaim our leadership towards the future."[56]

Browning's article arrived too late for Radhakrishnan to reply before the book was published. So I shall reply for him! I think he might have written, "I suppose I did use the concept of intuition loosely. But did I have good or bad intuitions? Perhaps intuitions ought to be examined axiologically rather than epistemologically."

2. His Lack of Consistency.

Many critics have called attention to Radhakrishnan's inconsistencies. For example, Clement C. J. Webb has pointed out that the word religion in Radhakrishnan's writings is used synonymously with faith, intuition, democracy, philosophy of change, and absolutism.[57] On pages 20-21 of The Bhagavadgītā[58] he used the following terms synonymously: "Ultimate Reality," "the Supreme," "Supreme Brahman," "Brahman," "God," "Spirit," "a sovereign unity," "the subsistent simplicity," "the pure subject," "the Self itself," "the universal knower," "the Eternal," "the Eternal One," "It," "the Supreme Identity," "the

Real," "the Absolute," "the one Reality," "the Supreme Self," "the ultimate principle," "the real self," "the God of worship," "the Divine Pattern," "the Universal Spirit," "*Paramātma*," "*Puruṣottama*," "The Supreme Person," "the uncaused cause," and "the unmoved mover." Such linguistic license can be tolerated in poetry; but philosophy, as the discipline is usually understood, requires sharper terminology.

Even more serious than linguistic carelessness are his occasional lapses in logic. Wadia notes "a bewildering conflict of statements, rendered all the more bewildering in Radhakrishnan by his habit of putting a certain facet of thought as forcibly as possible, leaving to others to make what they can of these contradictions."[59] For example, in a paper prepared as the opening address for "A Seminar on Saints" he wrote, "The awareness of the Supreme, the communion with the Absolute defies linguistic description or linguistic analysis. Each religious doctrine is an approximate statement, a symbolic description of the Absolute Reality."[60] In the first sentence of this paper he says the Absolute cannot be described, and in the second sentence he says the Absolute can be described! Of course, one could point out that contradictions are not unknown in *śruti* literature. *The Vedānta Sūtra* states both that the Brahman has *no* qualities and that the Brahman has *all* qualities—thus supporting the claims of both Śaṅkara and Rāmānuja. Śaṅkara was inconsistent, too. As Radhakrishnan says, "The anxiety to be loyal as far as possible to both Buddhism and Vedāntism appears to be the explanation of much of the inconsistency of Śaṅkara's philosophy. But there is no denying that the positive method Śaṅkara intends to pursue as a Vedāntin and the negative method he does sometimes pursue as an interpreter of Buddhism, end in conflict and contradiction."[61] But this does not justify Radhakrishnan's violation of the law of noncontradiction.

Radhakrishnan in his zeal to accomplish worthy ends sometimes made serious errors in elementary reasoning. D. G. Moses has called attention to the fact that, whereas in *The Hindu View of Life* on page 49 Radha-krishnan states that not all religious claims to reality are true—"Hinduism does not mistake tolerance for indiffer-ence. It affirms that while all revelation refers to reality, they are not equally true to it."—on page 58 of the same volume he argues for a "parliament," "commonwealth," or "federation" of religions as a solution to conflict on the ground that the claims of all religions are true.[62] Moses writes, "But what passes our comprehension is not that the same writer should suggest the idea of a parliament of religions as the solution of the problem of the conflict of religions. For the latter idea can only be based on a com-plete ignoring of the truth element in the different religions."[63]

Those who seek and find errors in reasoning in the writings of Radhakrishnan err in their assessment of the man. I keep coming back to his early book on Tagore, which he confessed was self-revelatory. Here is an excel-lent example: "Reason, which can help us to weigh the dust or measure the air, cannot show us the face of God. The truly religious soul does not argue and infer, but meditates and waits for light. The poet, the artist, and the lover pursue this path of intuition; the mystic knows it, and lives in the full light of the vision."[64] Radhakrishnan's conclusion with respect to Tagore was that he by "his power of imagination . . . breathed life into the dry bones of the ancient philosophy of India and made it live."[65] We may conclude with respect to Radhakrishnan that he tried to express these insights philosophically. Poetry is emotion remembered. Philosophy is experience reason-ed. "A true poet will be a philosopher, and a true philosopher will be a poet,"[66] wrote Radhakrishnan. Tagore was a philosophic poet. Radhakrishnan was a poetic philosopher. To those who accused him of illogi-calities, Radhakrishnan asserted, "Syllogism does not give us spirit."[67]

One of Radhakrishnan's most puzzling inconsisten-cies is his treatment of the concepts of the Absolute and God. Although he insists he is an Advaitin (nondualist), his language is often dualistic, for example, in *The Hindu View of Life* he writes that "we may not know God, but God certainly knows us."[68] No Advaitin could say that. No wonder some think he was a Viśiṣṭādvaitin.

Bhārati has written that the comparative philosopher is one who belongs "to the happier breed of thinkers who live without a system."[69] I do not think this is the case with Radhakrishnan, but I admit his "system" is sometimes difficult to identify. He said Tagore created an "atmosphere rather than a system of philosophy."[70] The same can be said of Radhakrishnan. The problem, of course, is that Radhakrishnan held positions as a professor of philosophy. Tagore did not.

P. T. Raju accuses Radhakrishnan of duplicity with respect to Indian philosophy. Raju writes that sometimes Radhakrishnan assumes "the self-sufficiency and self-completeness of Indian thought" and at other times complains of the incompleteness of Indian thought and shows "a desire to incorporate elements from Western thought."[71]

Again I insist we must pay attention to how Radhakrishnan perceived his life work. Perhaps we have paid too much attention to his role as an absolute idealist. He denied that he was either an epistemological idealist or an ontological idealist. The term he used first was "spiritual idealism." He wanted to put the ideal back into idealism. He might, therefore, be called "an axiological idealist." Not sufficient attention has been given by students of Indian philosophy to the value aspect of the Brahman. The term *ānanda* in *saccidānanda* refers to the objectivity of value rather than to joy, happiness, or bliss. What was Radhakrishnan trying to do? Note what he writes: "The supreme task of our generation is to give soul to world-consciousness."[72] "The transition that we have to effect today, if we are to survive, is a moral and spiritual revolution which should embrace the whole earth."[73]

Wadia offers an interesting explanation of Radhakrishnan's writings on Hinduism which may help us appreciate some of his inconsistencies. Wadia says that he went through three stages in his attitude toward Hinduism. There was first a period of youthful idealistic praise of Hinduism. Caste, for example, was "a great achievement." This period is the time in which he wrote *The Hindu View of Life* (1926). The second period was a time of greater maturity during which he attempted a philosophical justification of Hinduism. At this time he preferred to call caste "class." This period is seen in *Eastern Religions and Western Thought* (1939). The third period was a time of realistic evaluation. At this time he was "a bitter critic of the traditional caste system." The book of this period is *Religion and Society* (1947).[74]

I do not accept this explanation for all his logical looseness, but I think we must keep in mind that a philosopher who is committed to the life of reason and also to the life of a traditional religion may sometimes feel the tension of the two commitments: reason and revelation, evidence and faith, logic and love, head and heart.

Radhakrishnan made a great mistake in not going over his writings before his death—as Augustine did in his *Retractions*—in order to re-examine what he had written, and, perhaps, to destroy some of his early assessments of Indian life and thought.

3. His Neglect of Analysis.

A third criticism of Radhakrishnan's writings is that he neglects analysis. For example, in a lecture titled "Religion and Religions" given on July 8, 1936, which is a pamphlet of a series on World Fellowship Through Religion sponsored by the World Congress of Faiths, he says, "God is not an abstraction but a being." Then he leaves the proposition, moving on to other topics. But such a statement needs clarification, explanation, amplification. Such pontifications are unforgivable in a philosopher. The poet Tagore held, "Intellect revelling in distinctions and opposites can give us, in the words of Bradley, an unearthly ballet of bloodless categories which is no substitute for the concrete riches of life."[75] A philosopher, however, must make "distinctions and opposites." There is some truth in the broad generalization that the West distinguishes and the East diffuses.

Robert Minor begins his recent biographical study of Radhakrishnan by noting that many evaluations of the thought of Radhakrishnan are misleading because they are "normative philosophical analyses of the consistency, coherence and satisfactoriness of Radhakrishnan's thought in comparison with ideas from Indian and/or Western traditions."[76] Minor rightly calls attention to Radhakrishnan's claim that his thoughts are "born of spiritual experience."[77] But Radhakrishnan was a philosopher, and he knew that analysis is intrinsic to philosophy. He said in an address to the International Institute of Philosophy and the Indian Philosophical Congress in a meeting in Mysore on August 22, 1959, "Every great philosopher is both an analyst and an existentialist. He is a poet with an intellectual conscience. Analysis without vision, unexamined intuition, sheer passion are the sources of superstition, fanaticism, madness."[78] Unfortunately, Radhakrishnan's practice was not always consistent with these statements. His words here are worth more than his actions!

Arapura writes that he notes "a certain amount of alternation, confusion and lack of clearness"[79] in the writings of Radhakrishnan. One way of explaining this is to point out that Radhakrishnan as philosopher was more concerned about synthesis than about analysis. Philosophy, he said, is "an attempt to conceive of the world as a whole by means of thought."[80] He wrote that when he was appointed Professor of Philosophy at age 30 in the University of Mysore, he was persuaded that philosophy leads us to a spiritual or absolutistic view.[81] "The whole course of philosophy," he wrote, "is a continuous affirmation of the truth that insight into reality does not come through the analytic intellect."[82]

There is a humorous exchange dealing with analysis

in the volume on Radhakrishnan in *The Library of Living Philosophers*. Swāmi Agehānanda Bhārati in his contribution to that volume says his "main conclusion" is "that Professor Radhakrishnan is a theologian, and that he is the theologian of Hinduism."[83] The Swāmi adds "This is the highest tribute a monk can pay to a layman."[84] Of course, Bhārati, in referring to himself as "a monk" and to Radhakrishnan as "a layman," has pulled rank on Radhakrishnan. But, in addition, by calling Radhakrishnan a theologian he has denied that Radhakrishnan is a philosopher. Bhārati continues, "The philosopher wants to know what he can know and keeps a proper respect towards the unknowable; the theologian wants to describe what he cannot know by any discursive means, but he becomes discursive only after his premises have been established. He must invoke intuition and revelation as his final authority."[85] Radhakrishnan in his reply to Bhārati is for the most part dispassionate. But it is interesting to note that Radhakrishnan the layman refers to his critic with the holy title "Swāmiji." (One wonders if that was tongue in cheek!) Put even more humorously, Radhakrishnan—now a theologian!—retaliates by referring to "Swāmiji" as one who has been corrupted by logical positivism![86]

There is another aspect of the conflict between Bhārati and Radhakrishnan that should be mentioned. Bhārati says that one of the reasons why he holds Radhakrishnan to be a theologian rather than a philosopher is because Radhakrishnan seeks intellectual certainty. Surety, according to Bhārati, is the mark of a theologian, and doubt is the mark of a philosopher.[87] Bhārati argues, Radhakrishnan said, "Man cannot live on doubt,"[88] so Radhakrishnan cannot be a philosopher. Bhārati's logic, of course, depends upon the assumption that doubt is an essential tool in the philosopher's kit. If surety is the mark of a theologian, then Bertrand Russell the atheist, whose great concern was the quest for certainty of knowledge, was a theologian!

The essays of Radhakrishnan are a delight to read.

But I do not recommend them as a steady diet. I confess that after reading Radhakrishnan for several days I feel an urgency to turn to works by Ayer, Ryle, Austin, and Max Black. Synthesis without analysis finally has the impact of a fairy tale. Radhakrishnan's sweeping generalizations and utopian hopes tend to stray from the realities of human experience. He was a tender-hearted man. I wish he had been more tough-minded.

4. His Use of Platitudes.

Radhakrishnan rarely starts from identified assumptions, develops a rational argument, and arrives at an established conclusion. Many of his essays remind one of the poetry of Shelley, Keats, and Wordsworth. They do not go anywhere. They are collections of insights. Radhakrishnan said Tagore's work is "a sigh of the soul rather than a reasoned account of metaphysics."[89] The same can be said of some of Radhakrishnan's essays. They contain much sighing, some reasoning. Many are what is known in Sanskrit as *sūtravana* (a forest of quotations) which reveal his wide reading in Eastern and Western literature, history, and philosophy, but do not lead to a logical conclusion.

Saher calls attention to Radhakrishnan's platitudes. For example, within a few consecutive pages in *Religion in a Changing World* one finds the following:

"Mankind is on trial."[90]

"Nation states are too narrow for the modern world."[91]

"Life is a perpetual struggle between good and evil."[92]

"Man is too vain, too stupid to know himself."[93]

"The human condition has to be changed."[94]

"Every morning begins a new day."[95]

"We are makers of history."[96]

These statements are not very informative or original—to say the very least! Saher offers an interesting explanation for such platitudes. He says the reader of Radhakrishnan must keep in mind that he was a mystic. His so-called platitudes would indeed be only platitudes "were they not backed by the sincerity of his first-hand mystical experience. A platitude uttered straight from the heart ceases to be one."[97] According to Saher, "If you deny Radhakrishnan mystic-enlightenment (*Erleuchtung*)[98] then his philosophy is only a string of elegant sayings, a rosary of rather second-hand gems. His platitudes are so obvious that no writer would have dared to utter them had they not been forced from him by the overwhelming pressure of the genuine religious-mystical experience behind them."[99]

Radhakrishnan's friend, B. K. Mallik, also refers to Radhakrishnan's "intimate spiritual experiences"[100] and his "beloved Krishna."[101] But Radhakrishnan wrote little about his personal religious life. There is one place in his "Fragments of a Confession" in which he does appear to refer to a mystical experience: "While I was greatly stimulated by the minds of all those whom I have studied, my thought does not comply with any fixed traditional pattern. For my thinking had another source and proceeded from my own experience, which is not quite the same as what is acquired by mere study and reading. It is born of spiritual experience rather than deduced from logically ascertained premises.[102]

Other explanations are also in order. One is that he wrote too much, too fast, too frequently. In his various administrative positions he was constantly called upon to speak. He must have written his essays and addresses during moments when he was not engaged in official responsibilities. He wrote introductions to scores of books. C. E. M. Joad in his fascinating study of Radhakrishnan, *Counter Attack from the East*, says, "Much has been written of Radhakrishnan the thinker, but of Radhakrishnan the talker and listener not enough."[103] Joad notes something else about Radhakrishnan's writings and speaking: "He does not, except when he is very excited, mistake rhetoric for argument, or believe that the mere process of asserting something in a number of different and increasingly eloquent ways somehow makes it true."[104] But Radhakrishnan did sometimes mistake rhetoric for argument! We must keep in mind that he pursued the philosophical discipline not for philosophy's sake but as a means to accomplish the end nearest his heart. Radhakrishnan appears to have regarded what others called *platitudes* as *sūtras* (aphorisms) for the enlightenment and guidance of fellow human beings. They may be regarded as devices to assist men and women to *mokṣa*.

5. His Apologetic Style.

What was Radhakrishnan? Bhārati says he was a Hindu theologian.[105] Roy says he was not a Hindu.[106] Mallik says, "Most unmistakably I find him to be a Hindu above everything else and that is perhaps the only true and faithful description of him."[107] Browning says he was a poet.[108] Brightman says he was a preacher.[109] Mallik says he was a Saint.[110] S. K. Ray says he was "a complete mystic."[111] Saher says he was a holy sage and mystic.[112] Arapura says he was a politician.[113] Radhakrishnan classified himself as an apologist.[114] Minor, in the concluding chapter of his "religious biography" of Radhakrishnan writes, "Radhakrishnan's life was the life of an apologist. His defense of 'Hinduism' and India dominated all of his work."[115] M. N. Roy writes that the volume *The Hindu View of Life* is "much too apologetic to be a positive statement of Indian Philosophy."[116] I define his apology as three-fold: (1) Idealism as the only proper philosophy. (2) Hinduism as religion rather than as *a* religion. (3) India as the spiritual leader of the world.

He held that "all philosophy is idealistic" both in the East and in the West in holding to "the inseparability of the highest value from the truly real" and to "an ultimate connection of value and reality."[117] He wrote, "It is my opinion that systems which play the game of philosophy squarely and fairly, with freedom from presuppositions and religious neutrality, naturally end in absolute idealism; and if they lead to other conclusions, we may always suspect that the game has not been played according to the rules."[118]

He held that Hinduism is the religion of religions. He claimed that "half the world moves on independent foundations which Hinduism supplied."[119] He approved of Tagore's admonition "Cling to religion, let religions go."[120] Religions have little to do with religion. Hence, "The world will be a much more religious place if all the religions were removed from it."[121]

He held that India points the way to the spiritual ideal. He wrote, "India with her distinctive spiritual outlook can provide the world with the soul for which it is seeking."[122] "With its profound sense of spiritual reality brooding over the world of our ordinary experience, with its lofty insights and immortal aspirations, Indian thought may perhaps wean us moderns from a too exclusive occupation with secular life or with the temporary formulations in which logical thought has too often sought to imprison spiritual aspiration."[123]

In his "Fragments of a Confession" he notes that a "writer may at times allow his personal bias to determine his presentation."[124] In reading Radhakrishnan I often long for more critical thinking and less propaganda. There are few times in which he did not allow his personal bias to determine his presentation.

The notion that a philosopher can think without presuppositions is, of course, ridiculous. But one who always fails to examine his presuppositions is less than a philosopher. Radhakrishnan's propensity to defend idealism, Hinduism, and India is obvious. Radhakrishnan-the-poet-preacher-theologian-statesman-apologist-sage-mystic-saint sometimes makes it difficult to locate Radhakrishnan-the-philosopher. Saher thinks he had a vision. I agree. But I do not think it was a supernatural vision. It was a vision like Tagore's: a vision of *sarvamukti* (universal liberation). It was a vision of the entire world as an abode of peace. It was a vision of a physical world in which each finds a place. It was a vision of a spiritual world in which all respect the right of others to work out their own salvation.

Arapura observes that much of Radhakrishnan's written material "rings with the tones of election campaign speeches, rather than with those of philosophy."[125] That depends on how one defines philosophy. Radhakrishnan was certainly not an impartial philosopher. He defended spiritual idealism, democracy, international peace, Indian nationalism, and the Hindu religion. He rejected materialism, positivism, organized religions, and warfare.

What was Radhakrishnan? I find it helpful to compare him with Aurobindo. Aurobindo presented himself as a *guru*, and denied that he was a philosopher. Radhakrishnan presented himself as a philosopher, and denied that he was a *guru*. He wrote, "If we take any philosopher as a *guru*, if we treat his work as gospel, if we make of his teachings a religion complete with dogma and exegesis, we may become followers of the congregation of the faithful, but will not possess the openness of mind essential for a critical understanding of the master's views."[126] A flaw in the volume on Radhakrishnan in *The Library of Living Philosophers*, as the editor notes, is that because of "the very high esteem in which Radhakrishnan is held everywhere" a large number of the essays in the volume are "more eulogistic in character than critical or philosophically objective."[127] Yet, according to Radhakrishnan, "true teachers" as contrasted to *gurus* are those who "help us to think for ourselves."[128] In his commentary on the *Bhagavad Gītā* Radhakrishnan observes, "A true teacher does not assume a false responsibility. Even if the pupil takes a wrong turn, he would only counsel but not compel him to turn back, if such a procedure should interfere with his individual freedom of choice. . . . Teaching is not indoctrination."[129] Radhakrishnan admonishes on the teacher-pupil relationship: "We would be unworthy disciples if we do not question and criticize them."[130] We, who aspire to be worthy students of Radhakrishnan, therefore question and criticize him.

Notes

1. P. J. Saher, *Eastern Wisdom and Western Thought*. London: George Allen and Unwin, 1969, p. 51.

2. *The Philosophy of Sarvepalli Radhakrishnan*. Ed. Paul Arthur Schlipp. New York: Tudor Publishing Co., 1952, p. 3 Identified hereafter as *PSR*.

3. *Occasional Speeches and Writings. October 1952-February 1959*. New Delhi: The Publications Division, Ministry of Information and Broadcasting, Government of India, 1960, p. 422.

4. Ibid., p. 423.

5. *The Concept of Man*. Eds. S. Radhakrishnan and P. T. Raju. Lincoln, Nebraska: Johnsen Publishing Co., 1960, p. 11.

6. Saher, *Eastern Wisdom and Western Thought*, p. 50.

7. London: Kegan Paul, Trench, Trubner, 1929, p. 96.

8. *PSR*, p. xxi.

9. *The Philosophy of Rabindranath Tagore*. London: Macmillan, 1918. Identified hereafter as *PRT*.

10. "My Search for Truth" in *Religion in Transition*. Ed. Vergilius Ferm. London: George Allen and Unwin, 1937, p. 43.

11. T. R. V. Murti, "Writings of Sarvepalli Radhakrishnan to March, 1952" in *PSR*, p. 854.

12. "My Search for Truth" in *Religion in Transition*, pp. 12-13.

13. Ibid., p. 11.

14. Ibid.

15. Ibid., p. 44.

16. *PRT*, pp. 103-104.

17. London: George Allen and Unwin, 1927, p. 30.

18. Ibid.

19. Ibid., p. 99.

20. Ibid., p. 100.

21. "The Social Philosophy of Radhakrishnan" in *PSR*, p. 768.

22. Ibid., p. 769.

23. New Delhi: Orient Paperbacks, 1978, p. 20. A. N. Marlow says that Radhakrishnan wrote "with a sustained loftiness of aim." (*Radhakrishnan: An Anthology*. London: George Allen and Unwin, 1952, p. 5.)

24. Ibid.

25. London: George Allen and Unwin, 1933, p. 135.

26. P. 479.

27. "Fragments of a Confession" in *PSR*, p. 3.

28. *Modern Indian Thought*. Bombay: Asia Publishing House, 1964, p. 231. Naravane adds, "It must be admitted that in some of his works Radhakrishnan has laid himself open to the charge of ambiguity. Many of his remarks serve to stimulate and suggest rather than to prove a point; he seems to have made them with the awareness that what is lost in precision is gained in intensity and inspiration." (Ibid., p. 243.)

29. "Radhakrishnan and the Other Vedānta" in *PSR*, pp. 470-471.

30. London: Macmillan, 1920.

31. "My Search for Truth" in *Religion in Transition*, p. 24.

32. Ibid.

33. Ibid.

34. Ibid., p. 25.

35. "Radhakrishnan's World" in *PSR*, p. 87.

36. Ibid., p. 110.

37. Ibid.

38. Ibid.

39. *Eastern Wisdom and Western Thought*, p. 52.

40. "Radhakrishnan and Philosophy of the State and Community" in *PSR*, p. 731. He uses the word *Saint* with a capital S!

41. Second edition. London: George Allen and Unwin, 1937, p. 134.

42. "Reason and Intuition in Radhakrishnan's Philosophy" in *PSR*, pp. 177-178.

43. For example, "While outer knowledge can be easily acquired, inner truth demands an absolute concentration of the mind on its object. . . . The individual surrenders to the object and is absorbed by it. He becomes what he beholds. The distinction between subject and object disappears." *Eastern Religions and Western Thought*. London: Oxford University Press, 1939, p. 50.

44. My term, not Browning's.

45. Ibid., p. 181.

46. Ibid., p. 177.

47. Ibid.

48. "Reply to Critics" in *PSR*, p. 791.

49. *PRT*, p. 152.

50. Ibid., p. 160. Humayun Kabir says Radhakrishnan's political philosophy may "be summed up in one phrase as 'Enlightened Humanism.' " "Radhakrishnan's Political Philosophy" in *PSR*, p. 707.

51. *PSR*, p. 6.

52. "Radhakrishnan and Indian Civilization" in *Radhakrishnan. Comparative Studies in Philosophy Presented in Honour of His Sixtieth Birthday*. London: George Allen and Unwin, p. 262.

53. *Eastern Religions and Western Thought*, p. 23.

54. *Indian Philosophy*, Vol. 1. London: George Allen and Unwin, 1927, p. 37.

55. *Eastern Wisdom and Western Thought*, p. 17.

56. *PSR*, p. 842.

57. "Theism and Absolutism in Radhakrishnan's Philosophy" in *PSR*, pp. 385-386. Webb missed the use of *religion* as "an experience of reality" in "Religious Philosophy," *The Hibbert Journal*, Vol. 20, No. 1, October, 1921, p. 37. Radhakrishnan in *Education, Politics and War* (Poona: International Book Service, 1944, p. 8) writes that democracy is not merely "a fine political arrangement, but it is the highest religion."

58. London: George Allen and Unwin, 1948.

59. "The Social Philosophy of Radhakrishnan" in *PSR*, p. 777. M. A. Barth says that "no nation has shewn more indifference to contradictions than has India." (*Bulletin on the Religions of India*. Calcutta: Firma K. L. Mukhopadhyaya, 1960, p. 1.)

60. *A Seminar on Saints*. Ed. T. M. P. Mahadevan. Madras: Ganesh, 1960, p. 3.

61. *PRT*, pp. 116-117.

62. See David Gnanaprakasam Moses, *Religious Truth and the Relation between Religions*. Madras: The Christian Literature Society for India, 1950, pp. 117-121.

63. Ibid., pp. 120-121.

64. *PRT*, p. 45.

65. Ibid., p. 119.

66. Ibid., p. 165.

67. Ibid., p. 37. E. A. Burtt accuses the West of "a semi-deification of the law of contradiction." ("What can Western Philosophy Learn from India?" *Philosophy East and West*, Vol. 5, No. 3 [1955], p. 206.) Fritjof Capra says that a great danger in the human condition is that "the rational mind can detach itself from the human being and not feel things intuitively." ("*The Tao of Physics* Revisited" in *The Holographic Paradigm and Other Paradoxes*. Ed. Ken Wilber. Boulder: Shambhala, 1982, p. 230.

68. P. 50.

69. "Radhakrishnan and the Other Vedānta" in *PSR*, p. 464.

70. *PRT*, p. 6.

71. "Radhakrishnan's Influence on Indian Thought" in PSR, pp. 522-523.

72. *Eastern Religions and Western Thought*, p. viii.

73. *Occasional Speeches and Writings. July 1959-May 1962.* New Delhi: The Publications Division, Ministry of Information and Broadcasting, Government of India, 1963, p. 211.

74. "The Social Philosophy of Radhakrishnan" in *PSR*, pp. 760, 766.

75. *PRT*, p. 152.

76. *Radhakrishnan. A Religious Biography.* Albany: State University of New York Press, 1987, p. 1.

77. "Fragments of a Confession" in *PSR*, p. 10.

78. *Occasional Speeches and Writings. July 1959-May 1962*, p. 257.

79. *Radhakrishnan and Integral Experience.* London: Asia Publishing House, 1966, p. 27. Thomas Paul Urumpackal in *Organized Religion According to Dr. S. Radhakrishnan* (Rome: Università Gregoriana Editrice, 1972, pp. 208-222) lists many of Radhakrishnan's misinterpretations of Hinduism and Christianity, erroneous quotations, and other errors.

80. *PRT*, p. 163.

81. "My Search for Truth" in *Religion in Transition*, p. 24.

82. Ibid., p. 23.

83. "Radhakrishnan and the Other Vedānta" in *PSR*, p. 465.

84. Ibid.

85. Ibid., p. 469.

86. "Reply to Critics" in *PSR*, p. 816.

87. "Radhakrishnan and the Other Vedānta" in *PSR*, p. 464.

88. *Indian Philosophy*, Vol. 2, p. 19.

89. *Ibid.*, p. 6.

90. London: George Allen and Unwin, 1967, p. 29.

91. Ibid., p. 21.

92. Ibid., p. 31.

93. Ibid., p. 30.

94. Ibid., p. 32.

95. Ibid., p. 33.

96. Ibid.

97. *Eastern Wisdom and Western Thought*, p. 52.

98. The German word *Erleuchtung* is the approximate equivalent of *mokṣa*, that is, "salvation," "liberation," "self-realization," "the *tat tvam asi* experience."

99. *Eastern Wisdom and Western Thought*, p. 52.

100. "Radhakrishnan and Indian Civilization" in *Radhakrishnan. Comparative Studies in Philosophy Presented in Honour of His Sixtieth Birthday*, p. 262.

101. Ibid., p. 264.

102. *PSR*, p. 10. Edgar Sheffield Brightman says of Radha-krishnan, "If he is a mystic, he is not autobiographical. We search in vain for introspective confessions." ("Radhakrish-nan and Mysticism" in *PSR*, p. 394.)

103. London: George Allen and Unwin, 1933, p. 38.

104. Ibid., p. 40.

105. "Radhakrishnan and the Other Vedānta" in *PSR*, p. 465.

106. "Radhakrishnan in the Perspective of Indian Philosophy" in *PSR*, p. 548.

107. "Radhakrishnan and Indian Civilization" in *Radha-krishnan. Comparative Studies in Philosophy Presented in Honour of His Sixtieth Birthday*, p. 258.

108. "Reason and Intuition in Radhakrishnan's Philosophy" in *PSR*, p. 177.

109. "Radhakrishnan and Mysticism" in *PSR*, p. 394.

110. "Radhakrishnan and Philosophy of the State and Community" in *PSR*, p. 731.

111. *The Political Thought of President Radhakrishnan*. Calcutta: Firma K. L. Mukhopadhyaya, 1966, p. 5. Ray inor-dinately states, "Radhakrishnan, the greatest living philosopher of India and one of the foremost of humanity, is at the same time one of the most cultured men of the epoch. A man in intellect and courage, yet without conceit or bravado; a saint in purity of life and devotion of heart, yet without asceticism or religiosity; a prince (president) in dignity and courtesy, yet without formality or condescension; a scholar in tastes and habits, yet without aloofness or bookishness; a knight-errant in hatred of wrong and contempt of baseness, yet without self-righteousness or cynicism; a philosopher in thought and feeling, yet without affectation; a patriot yet without prejudice or complex—he unites in his strong transparent humanity many unique qualities." (Ibid., p. 16.)

112. *Eastern Wisdom and Western Thought*, p. 51. Rama Shanker Srivastava writes, "Radhakrishnan is a mystic philosopher. His religious experiences serve as data to his philosophy. He depends more on his experiences and inspira-tions than on his study." (*Contemporary Indian Philosophy*. Delhi: Munshi Ram Manchar Lal, 1965, p. 258.)

113. *Radhakrishnan and Integral Experience*, p. 23.

114. "Fragments of a Confession" in *PSR*, p. 11.

115. *Radhakrishnan. A Religious Biography*, p. 137.

116. "Radhakrishnan in the Perspectives of Indian Philosophy" in *PSR*, p. 545.

117. P. 16.

118. *The Reign of Religion in Contemporary Philosophy.* London: Macmillan, 1920, p. vii. One must not read too much into Radhakrishnan's use of *idealism*. For example, in *An Idealist View of Life* (London: George Allen and Unwin, 1929, p. 18) he writes, "An idealist view of life only contends that the universe has meaning, has value. Ideal values are dynamic forces; they are the driving power of the universe. The world is intelligible only as a system of ends. Such a view has nothing to do with the problem of whether a thing is only a particular image or a general relation."

119. *The Hindu View of Life,* p. 16.

120. *PRT,* pp. 108-109.

121. *An Idealist View of Life,* p. 45.

122. *Is This Peace?* Second edition. Bombay: Hind Kitabs, 1946, p. 72.

123. "Fragments of a Confession" in *PSR,* p. 7.

124. *PSR,* p. 11.

125. *Radhakrishnan and Integral Experience,* p. 23.

126. "Fragments of a Confession" in *PSR,* p. 8.

127. Preface to *PSR,* p. xii.

128. "Fragments of a Confession" in *PSR,* p. 8.

129. *The Bhagavadgītā.* Second edition. London: George Allen and Unwin, 1963, p. 376.

130. "Fragments of a Confession" in *PSR,* p. 8.

Part Two
The Ways of Oneness of East and West with Special Reference to Radhakrishnan

One afternoon during the last week of the Second East-West Philosophers' Conference at the University of Hawaii in Honolulu in the summer of 1949 the Director of the Conference, Charles A. Moore, called a meeting of the nonpanel members to inform us that a new journal to be called *Philosophy East and West* would soon be launched. He invited us to submit articles for publication. I recall that I was puzzled why the journal was to be called *Philosophy East and West* rather than *Philosophy East-West*. But I decided the choice between hyphen and conjunctive was too trivial to discuss. Now— almost forty years later—I think the issue worth consideration.

There were other East-West conferences in Honolulu. There were no West-East conferences. Moore often referred to Hawaii as a place where one went west to get to the East and went east to get to the West. The first East-West conference was in 1939. Only a few philosophers from Japan, China, India, and the West shared ideas from their respective philosophies. The second conference was a much larger gathering. Appreciation and understanding of each other prevailed during the six weeks. The third conference, which was held in 1959, was marred by many efforts to refute one another. At one point the Indian delegation threatened to leave. The 1964 conference attempted to deal with one topic: the individual in Eastern and Western philosophy, but there

was little agreement on what the concept *individual*
denoted, designated, and connoted. Moore told me several years later that he remembered the 1949 conference
with great satisfaction, and that he was less pleased with
the other conferences.

East-West conferences in Honolulu and elsewhere
have helped many philosophers to shift in their thinking
from East versus West to East and West. Today a few
philosophers engage in WEST- east or EAST-west thinking, that is, in philosophizing which takes into some account the philosophies of the other hemisphere, although
with many doubts about what those from the other hemisphere may contribute. Only a very few engage in thinking that recognizes the credibility of both Eastern and
Western philosophy. Many students in Western colleges
and universities are still informed that Thales was the
first philosopher.

How the rational animal became separated into East
and West is not a major concern of philosophers.
Originally all human beings were Easterners or Westerners—or perhaps Southerners or Northerners. Long
before the Common Era human beings began to be
curious about people in other parts of the world. Egypt
was one place where a few from the East and a few from
the West met for comparative studies. Greece remained
complacently self-centered. Non-Hellenes were barbarians. The Greeks allegorized the conflict between
civilization and barbarians in battles between Lapiths
and Centaurs. An early breakthrough occurred when
Alexander the Great, going counter to his teacher, Aristotle, who advised that non-Greeks be treated like vege-
tables, went to India as part of an ambitious plan to mix
East and West like wine and water in a krater. Alexander,
be it noted, knew which were "wine" and which were
"water."

Megasthenes, a Greek sent in c. 300 B.C.E. to India by
Seleucis, the Monarch of Syria, reported that the Indian
philosophers, whom he called *gymnosophists* (naked

wisemen), held opinions which at some points almost coincided with those held by Greek philosophers.

Sarvepalli Radhakrishnan, the best-known comparative philosopher of this century, claims that "since the dawn of reflection the dream of unity has hovered over the scene and haunted the imagination."[1] But he does not furnish evidence or argument for this happy pontification. P. Kodanda Rao thinks that the unity of humanity is a fact, not a dream: "Civilization is one and is indivisible into Eastern and Western; its elements are a function ever of time, decreasingly of space but never of race."[2]

Hopes for world unity followed both World Wars. After World War I the League of Nations was formed to implement the aspirations for international peace and cooperation. Wendell Willkie's *One World* (1943), which was published in the middle of World War II, evidences the dream of a world unity. The forming of the United Nations in 1945 was another attempt to realize world oneness. Unfortunately, the deaths of millions of men and women were the catalyst for these two efforts.

The horrors of the two great wars make Radhakrishnan's statement of 1952 seem unrealistic: "The prominent feature of our time is not so much the wars and dictatorships which have disfigured it, but the emergence of a new civilization based on the truths of the spirit and the unity of mankind."[3] He expressed the same optimism in 1960—this time specifically about philosophy: "One of the chief features of philosophical thought today is the growing universality of outlook. Even Western thinkers are slowly giving up their provincial outlook and are admitting that thinkers outside their cultural traditions have grappled with the central problems of philosophy and a study of their writings may be helpful to students of philosophy."[4]

In 1967 Radhakrishnan was even more euphoric: "The human race is one. We stand on the threshold of a new society, a single society."[5] While no one would disagree with the factuality of the first statement, nor object to the hope expressed in the second statement, few would agree with Radhakrishnan when he went on to say, "East and West are relative terms. They are geographical expressions and do not represent cultural types."[6]

P. J. Saher wrote in 1969, "Mankind is entering a new phase of evolution, a phase of a higher dimension of consciousness. The distinction between Eastern and Western, American and Chinese philosophy will very soon become a thing of the past. The philosophy of the future will be an integral one regardless of the place where the body of the person setting forth his thoughts happened to be born."[7]

According to Radhakrishnan "When we take a long view of history we will find that there is not an Eastern view which is different from the Western view of life."[8] But he did not indicate how long the "long view" must be! I suspect one would need to go back into pre-history to locate this idyllic state. It is amusing to note that on the same page on which Radhakrishnan makes this sweeping statement he deplores the use of sweeping statements.[9]

The belief that a Western scholar might profit from the study of Eastern thought is largely a phenomenon of the late nineteenth and the twentieth centuries. The editors of the volume published in 1951 to honor Radhakrishnan on his sixtieth birthday wrote in the Introduction: "Less than a century ago there was no serious eagerness for a shared understanding between East and West except among grammarians and philologists, together with a few unusually broad-minded missionaries."[10] The concept of comparative philosophy was first formulated in a doctoral dissertation in the early 1920s at the Sorbonne by Paul Masson-Oursel. He understood comparative philosophy as the drawing of analogies of relationships. For example, karma is to Indian thought as the problem of determinism versus free will is to Western thought. A comparative philosopher, as conceived at that time, might have an appreciation of another system of philosophy and yet have no desire to incorporate any of that system into his own philosophy. A philosopher might merely recognize the legitimacy of another philosophy from another part of the globe. This is an admirable trait for a philosopher to have, but it is not the relationship examined in this study of the ways of oneness.

By the time of Masson-Oursel's dissertation two Indian intellectuals had already moved much further into comparative studies, holding that "there is neither East nor West in the realm of the spirit."[11] The two were the poet Rabindranath Tagore (1861-1941) and the philosopher Sarvepalli Radhakrishnan (1888-1975). C. E. M. Joad believed that Radhakrishnan was "peculiarly fitted by nature and training to mediate between East and West."[12] The same can be said of Tagore. Both were equally at home in India and in Europe.

Later in the twentieth century comparative philosophy outgrew the stage in which it was pursued largely to satisfy historical interest or exotic curiosity. Eliot Deutsch neatly states the newer motivation: it is becoming apparent "that we are ready to pursue new goals in comparative philosophy and to bring comparative philosophy into the mainstream of *creative* thought— East and West. ... Students ought to be able to study Asian thought simply for the purpose of enriching their philosophical background and enabling them to deal better with the philosophical problems that interest them."[13]

The editors of the sixtieth birthday volume referred to Radhakrishnan as "heir of the great Indian tradition" and master of "the Oriental perspective." They said he had achieved a "synthesis of attitudes and cultural approaches."[14] They found four themes in Radhakrishnan's books and lectures: "the primacy of spiritual values,"[15] "the lack and necessity of the spiritual note in modern civilization,"[16] "the logical inevitability of a spiritual absolutism in philosophy,"[17] and "the undeniable truth of our inner life or spirit."[18]

The words *spiritual* and *spirit* are significant. A key question to put to Radhakrishnan is a request for a full definition of *spiritual*. A partial answer is that, since *spiritual* is the opposite of *material*, the term denotes the goods of life which may be said to be nonmaterial. However, there is a clue in the statement of the fourth theme. Spirit is coupled with the inner life, so spiritual values are those values associated with the private life of a human being. Although "inner life" might refer to aesthetic, or moral, or intellectual, or religious values, Radhakrishnan uses the term largely to refer to religious values. Western civilization, according to his interpretation, added the life of the spirit to the three chief Greek ideals, namely, rationalistic philosophy, humanistic ethics, and nationalistic politics. However, the life of the spirit deteriorated into scholasticism, dogma, and an authoritative religious-political hierarchy. According to the editors of the sixtieth birthday volume, Radhakrishnan "believes that the philosophies of the East, and of India in particular, have from the beginning upheld the spiritual tradition."[19] The editors almost parrot the words of Radhakrishnan when they write, "The East has come to realize that for the preservation of its own values, and for assuring them a broader and stabler base, Western science must be mastered. . . . The West has begun to realize that there are spiritual depths in the Orient which it has not yet plumbed, and that if these were understood a way could be found to overcome its frantic competitiveness and achieve the inner and outer peace it has hitherto lacked."[20] Radhakrishnan never wavered in his assessment of which has the greater need. The East is deficient in means. The West lacks goals. The editors state, "His main and central teaching is that the spiritual should be given primacy; and reason and humanism, or science and man, should be explained in the light of the spiritual."[21]

Perhaps one of the best insights into Radhakrishnan's understanding of the spiritual is found in the General Introduction to *A Source Book in Indian Philosophy*. He writes that the "chief mark" of Indian philosophy is "its concentration upon the spiritual."[22] He devotes a paragraph to the explanation of this "chief mark," and, although he uses the term *spiritual* ten times, he offers no definition. One can gather, however, that *spiritual* means ontologically nonphysical and axiologically nonmaterial, from this statement: "Neither man nor universe is looked upon as physical in essence, and material welfare is never recognized as the goal of human life, except by the Cārvāka."[23] He notes later, "The future of civilization depends upon the return of spiritual awareness to the hearts and minds of men."[24] But if *spiritual* means nonphysical and nonmaterial, does he believe that the future of civilization depends upon ceasing to be concerned about food, clothing, shelter, medicine, communication, transportation, agriculture, and engineering? What a strangely unrealistic view! This reminds me of the Jesuit university that forgot to include plans for toilets in its blueprints for a new classroom building!

I think Radhakrishnan should have limited *spiritual* to axiology. For example, he might have stated that *spiritual* designates sharability. Unshareable goods are limited such that one's possession limits another's possession. Land ownership is an example. Shareable goods are unlimited. Scholarship is an example. Gilbert Murray has no monopoly on mastery of Greek drama!

When I read Radhakrishnan's emphasis on the spirituality of modern India, I wonder how well Radhakrishnan knew modern India. Did he not hear the wails of street beggars? Did he never see a hungry person sorting through garbage for scraps of food? And as for Hindu spirituality, one careful observer reports, "Most Hindus now are not particularly concerned with matters of the spirit."[25]

Radhakrishnan not only defended spirituality but also idealism. Often he coupled the two as "spiritual idealism." D. M. Datta says that *An Idealist View of Life* "can be regarded as the first grand experiment on the constructive side of comparative philosophy."[26] Radhakrishnan adopted and adapted idealism as the method of doing comparative philosophy. He wrote, "In a sense, as Hegel said, all philosophy is idealistic. In contrasting appearance and reality, fact and truth, existence and essence, it is led to admit an ideal world beyond the phenomenal.

Even absolute materialism is idealism, though of a crude form, for the matter to which all existence is reduced is not concrete reality but an abstract idea."[27]

I cannot decide whether Radhakrishnan's interest in religion led him to an idealistic position or whether a conviction of the truth of idealism led him to do comparative philosophy largely through the analysis of religion.

Sometimes Radhakrishnan makes a distinction between intuition and intelligence similar to that of Northrop in *The Meeting of East and West*. For example, he writes in *An Idealist View of Life*, "While the dominant feature of Eastern thought is its insistence on creative intuition, the Western systems are generally characterized by a greater adherence to critical intelligence."[28] But Radhakrishnan cautions that the distinction between Eastern intuition and Western intelligence is "only a question of emphasis."[29] Unfortunately at this crucial point Radhakrishnan reveals the inconsistency which is often found in his writings. Only four pages following he claims "the history of Western philosophy has been a supreme illustration of the primacy of the logical."[30] This is one of the places where Radhakrishnan-the-essayist displaces Radhakrishnan-the-philosopher. J. G. Arapura asserts that "the doctrines of distinctions and unity get very mixed up in his [Radhakrishnan's] mind."[31] This is a serious charge against Radhakrishnan's claim to be a philosopher. Philosophy is the science of making distinctions. In *Kalki; or, The Future of Civilization* Radhakrishnan pleads for "the fostering of oneness of thoughts and feeling among the human race."[32] One must remember in reading Radhakrishnan that in his writing he was usually more concerned about the impact on general readers than about the possible attack of analytic philosophers.

The first question to be asked in comparative philosophy is "What is the correct interpretation of interpretation?" Take Kant's *Critique of Pure Reason* as an example. Is it best understood in isolation from all other philosophical texts? How important is it to relate Kant to Hume? Is the state of European science in the eighteenth century a factor in understanding Kant? How important is it to relate Kant to the state of Christianity in Germany at the time of the composition of the book? And can the work be better understood if one relates it to Advaita Vedāntism and Mādhyamika Buddhism?

Harold McCarthy in an article titled "The Problem of Philosophical Diversity"[33] argues that the problems of philosophical diversity must be examined and a decision reached before entering the arena of relating Eastern and Western philosophies. He says there are ten options of interpretations:

1. There is one and only one interpretation.
2. All interpretations are inherently the same.
3. All interpretations are the same in essentials.
4. Each interpretation is at least partially true.
5. All interpretations are true relatively.
6. All intellectualized interpretations are false.
7. All nonscientific interpretations are meaningless.
8. All interpretations are historically meaningful and explicable.
9. Philosophizing must be done within a unified world framework.
10. All interpretations are equally possible.

D. M. Datta approaches the problem of relating Eastern and Western philosophies by suggesting six ways by which conflict may be overcome:

1. By accepting one theory as true and rejecting the other theory as false.
2. By partial acceptance and partial rejection of both theories.
3. By accepting both theories in a new light, realizing the complementary nature of their inner truths.
4. By rejecting both theories as based on a common wrong proposition, for example, William James replaced pessimism and optimism by substituting the term *meliorism*.
5. By rejecting the underlying problem itself as undecidable, illegitimate, self-contradictory, or meaningless.

6. By the self-negation of reason in favor of some superior self-manifest experience.[34]

The conventional term in East-West philosophical discussions in the 1950s was *synthesis*. When the journal *Philosophy East and West* was launched in 1951 the editor, Charles A. Moore, asked three well-known philosophers for a short statement on "philosophical synthesis." What he received was, no doubt, less than he had hoped. John Dewey wrote that there can be no "synthesis of East and West" because there is no "such a thing as 'West' and 'East' that have to synthesized."[35] Radhakrishnan wrote that what is needed is not "mergence" of East and West but "cross-fertilization" in which each "will retain its integrated structure."[36] George Santayana wrote that "synthesis" could only be achieved "by blurring or emptying both systems in what was clear and distinct in their results."[37] Santayana concluded, "From a literary and humanistic point of view I think that it is the *variety* and *incomparability* of systems, as of kinds of beauty, that makes them interesting, not any compromise or fusion that could be made of them."[38] In the same issue Paul Masson-Oursel argued that the only "true philosophy" is "comparative philosophy."[39] J. Kwee Swan Liat of the University of Sweden wrote that he saw "tendencies toward a universal philosophy" which will require "a conscious and repeated effort aimed at a merging of supplementary phases into an ever-rich totality where specific characteristics are not neglected but maintained and yet coherently connected."[40] A. C. Mukerji of the University of Allahabad, writing also in those halcyon days, stated that "the aim of philosophy has always been to realize the ideal whole which knows no temporal or spatial limits."[41] But Mukerji offered no guidelines other than "to follow the inner movement of thought in the Eastern and Western philosophical systems."[42] The ecstatic peak of that first year of the journal was a four-and-a-half-page article in the fourth number by Arnold H. Kamiat in which the words *synthesis* and *synthesize* appear twenty-one times. The article ends with this specimen of utopian nonsense: "And so, to conclude, the synthesis of East and West is to be effected, if at all, not by Easterners as such, or Westerners as such, but by those who adopt the attitude of intellectual universalism, transcend the limitations of Eastern and Western thought, and, employing objective procedures, seek to join, not East to West, but truth to truth."[43]

The subtitle of the volume containing the papers and seminar reports of the Second East-West Philosophers' Conference is *An Attempt at World Philosophical Synthesis*. The possibility of a synthesis of Eastern and Western philosophies was discussed *ad nauseam* in the early issues of *Philosophy East and West*, for example,

Kurt Leidecker	(Vol. 1, No. 2, 1951, pp. 40-50.)
William H. Sheldon	(Vol. 1, No. 3, 1951, pp. 3-6.)
D. T. Suzuki	(Vol. 1, No. 3, 1951, pp. 6-7.)
S. N. Dasgupta	(Vol. 1, No. 4, 1952, pp. 3-4.)
A. C. Mukerji	(Vol. 1, No. 4, 1952, pp. 4-5.)
Arnold H. Kamiat	(Vol. 1, No. 4, 1952, pp. 41-44.)
Giuseppe Tucci	(Vol. 2, No. 1, 1952, p. 3.)
William Ernest Hocking	(Vol. 2, No. 2, 1952, pp. 99-100.)
C. T. K. Chari	(Vol. 2, No. 3, 1952, pp. 187-207.)
Alan W. Watts	(Vol. 3, No. 2, 1953, pp. 99-100.)
J. Kwee Swan Liat	(Vol. 3, No. 2, 1953, pp. 101-116.)
S. K. Maitra	(Vol. 3, No. 3, 1953, pp. 195-198.)

The emphasis on synthesis was, I suspect, a response to Indian philosophy, to Hinduism, and, perhaps, even to Radhakrishnan. Radhakrishnan opines, "As contrasted with Western philosophy, with its analytic approach to reality and experience, Indian philosophy is fundamentally synthetic."[44] Radhakrishnan, says Suniti Kumar Chatterji, presents a "Dynamic Hinduism, which, true to its original character as a synthesis of diverse faiths and philosophies of life, is now offered as a Universal Doctrine capable of embracing the whole of humanity—as a *Sanātana Dharma* or 'Perennial Philosophy'—on which the wisdom and experience of the nations in the domain of the spiritual converge."[45] Any world philosophical synthesis, so characterized, would need to be a *super-synthesis*! No wonder some of the contacts in the early years of East-West philosophical discussions were regarded by some of the Indian philosophers as "mere hand-shaking."[46]

The term *meeting* was the preferred term prior to the popularity of *synthesis*. F. S. C. Northrop's study, *The Meeting of East and West*, fixed the term in the minds of many. Meetings can be of many varieties: from casual to intimate, from recognitions of another's presence to profound understanding and appreciation. The question is "What sort of meeting can there be between East and West?" Radhakrishnan wrote in 1939, "For the first time in the history of our planet its inhabitants have become one whole, each and every part of which is affected by the fortunes of each other. Science and technology, without aiming at this result, have achieved the unity. Economic and political phenomena are increasingly imposing on us the obligation to treat the world as a unit."[47] "The differences are fascinating but subordinate; the unity is the reality."[48] "The supreme task of our generation" said Radhakrishnan, "is to give a soul to the growing world-consciousness, to develop ideals and institutions necessary for the creative expression of the world soul, to transmit these loyalties and impulses to future generations and train them into world citizens."[49] He also spoke of the need for "a human consciousness of community."[50]

Well-meaning people sometimes claim that the oneness of East and West will not be difficult. The East will become more scientific. The West will become more religious. The result will be a unified East-West. As a warning against such facile optimism I place in opposition two statements from professors of philosophy, one from Baroda (India) and one from Minnesota (USA): "The West will yet have to accept the idea of *karma* and rebirth."[51] The "doctrine of reincarnation" [that is, *karma* and rebirth] is "a kind of doctrinal Himalaya between the West and India."[52]

Some of the accounts of the East-West situation written in the 1930s now appear pathetically humorous. For example, Joad wrote in 1933, "The West has the energy and vitality of a civilization comparatively young, yet does not know into what channels to direct them. . . . The East possesses the tradition and the knowledge, but is without the vitality to make the tradition live or the knowledge spread."[53] I fail to see what is accomplished by characterizing the West as young and stupid, and the East as old and feeble!

"The mind of the world must be pulled together."[54] So claimed Radhakrishnan in his "Fragments of a Confession." I discern two facets of that objective: (1) the nature of the goal, and (2) the means to the goal.

The goals of human life have been interestingly catalogued by Robert S. De Ropp in his book *The Master Game*.[55] De Ropp calls a life plan a "game," and delineates nine "games" of life, each with a distinctive goal:

1. The Master Game.	Goal = awakening to self-knowledge.
2. The Religion Game.	Goal = salvation from destruction.
3. The Science Game.	Goal = acquisition of knowledge.
4. The Art Game.	Goal = appreciation of beauty.
5. The Householder Game.	Goal = rearing a family.
6. No Game.	Goal = no aim, just existence.
7. The Hog in Trough Game.	Goal = wealth and physical enjoyments.
8. The Cock on Dunghill Game.	Goal = fame.
9. The Molock Game.	Goal = glory or victory.

For many historical reasons, which need not be enumerated or examined here, Easterners, reared in the traditions of Hinduism, Buddhism, Confucianism, and Taoism, tend to perceive life in terms of "The Master Game" and/or "The Religion Game"; whereas Westerners reared in the traditions of Judaic-Christianity—and especially the Westerner whose ancestors emigrated to the Americas—tend to perceive life in terms of wealth, physical enjoyments, fame, glory, and victory over natural elements and human enemies. The goals of Easterners and Westerners have been "pulled together" since World War II as people of the East enter the fields of industry and commerce and as people of the West experience doubts about the possibility or wisdom of endless material expansion.

The means, ways, or paths leading to the realization of life goals have been catalogued within Hinduism. The term *mārga* is used for the path to the goal of *mokṣa* (liberation, salvation, freedom from extinction, emancipation from the bondage of existence). According to Hinduism there are four principal *mārgas*:

1. *bhakti mārga*—the path of devotion.
2. *jñāna mārga* —the path of knowledge.
3. *karma mārga*—the path of moral action.
4. *yoga mārga* —the path of psycho-physical disciplines.

The question constantly raised by Hinduism is whether there is a pristine path, an *ēkata mārga* (a path of oneness). Buddhists also refer to a path or way (*yāna*) and disagree as to whether there is an *ekayāna* (a single path) and also as to whether the correct *yāna* is public (*Mahāyāna*) or private (*Hīnayāna*).

I contend there are eight principal ways to the oneness of East and West. They are Annihilation, Assimilation, Domination, Accommodation, Integration, Synthesis, Polarization, Omegalization. As a technique of clarification I shall list under each principal way words and phrases having an analogous or near-synonymous nature.

The authors of *Webster's New Dictionary of Synonyms*[56] protest against the "loosening" of the definition of *synonym* "within the last fifty or sixty years."[57] A loose definition, they insist, "is destructive of all the values that have come to be recognized as synonyms."[58] Hence, they offer a definition in which they claim "none of the loopholes may be left through which some synonymists have escaped."[59] Their definition is the following: "A synonym in this dictionary, will always mean one of two or more words in the English language which have the same or very nearly the same essential meaning."[60] I find the definition ludicrous. Do they believe that a word has only one synonym? Does not "very nearly the same essential meaning" introduce into their definition the "loosening" they deplore? And why use the word *essential*? I much prefer the nonstrict or usual definition given in *The Oxford English Dictionary* (1933 edition): "strictly, a word having the same sense as another (in the same language); but more usually, either or any of two or more words (in the same language) having the same general sense, but possessing each of them meanings which are not shared by the other or the others, or having different shades of meaning or implications appropriate to different contexts." The emphasis on the contextual aspects of words in the Oxford definition is important. The authors of the Merriam dictionary, recognizing that many people would use the book "as a word finder or as a vocabulary builder,"[61] decided to add lists of "analogous words."[62] Then, in another curious loosening, they state, "Some of the analogous words or terms closely related in meaning merit the name of near synonyms."[63]

I now list some "analogous words" or "near synonyms" of the eight ways of oneness:

ANNIHILATION. Abate. Abolish. Abrogate. Annul. Blot out. Confute. Convert. Defeat. Demolish. Destroy. Devastate. Disarm. Displace. Dispose. Eliminate. End. Erase. Exclude. Expunge. Extinguish. Ignore. Impair. Impose. Impoverish. Kill. Liquidate. Make impotent. Make nonexistent. Negate. Neutralize. Nullify. Obliterate. Ravage. Reject. Replace. Repudiate. Sack. Slaughter. Smash. Subrate. Terminate. Wreck.

ASSIMILATION. Absorb. Adapt. Adopt. Appropriate. Blend. Borrow. Combine. Commingle. Conform. Consume. Contain. Dissolve. Embody. Embrace. Identify with. Imitate. Include. Incorporate. Lose identity to. Make uniform. Merge. Mix. Reconcile. Reduce one to another. Reinterpret. Submerge.

DOMINATION. Assume superiority over. Become sovereign over. Coerce. Command. Control. Defeat. Govern. Influence. Lord over. Master. Moderate. Oppress. Overpower. Overthrow. Persecute. Prevail over. Propagandize. Restrain. Rule over. Subdue. Subordinate. Subjugate. Surpass. Sway. Take captive. Take control over. Take possession of. Take supremacy over.

ACCOMMODATION. Accord. Adjust. Allow to exist. Allow to remain. Analogize. Attune. Acknowledge parallels to. Compare. Compromise. Conduct dialogue with. Conform. Cooperate. Equalize. Concord. Have fellowship with. Fit into one another. Give into. Make provision for. Meet as equals. Modify. Notice. Pacify. Recognize. Reconceive. Reconcile. Reinterpret. Point to similarities. Provide a place for. Show charity to. Take a liberal attitude to. Take an open-minded attitude toward. Tolerate. Understand.

INTEGRATION. Agree. Amalgamate. Associate. Bind together. Blend. Bridge. Bring together. Come together. Complete. Comprehend. Conjoin. Connect. Consolidate. Concatenate. Converge. Correlate. Cross-fertilize. Embrace. Entwine. Establish a rapprochement. Establish harmonious relationships. Focus. Fuse. Harmonize. Homogenize. Incorporate. Include. Influence mutually. Intermingle. Interrelate. Interweave. Join together. Link together. Make parallel to. Mediate. Merge. Mesh. Mix. Perfect by relating parts or by adding parts. Reconcile. Relate. Unite so as to produce a mixture.

SYNTHESIS. Coalesce. Combine from elements. Combine in coalition. Compound. Comprehend into a unit. Configurate. Coordinate parts into a whole. Form a

SYNTHESIS. Coalesce. Combine from elements. Combine in coalition. Compound. Comprehend into a unit. Configurate. Coordinate parts into a whole. Form a gestalt. Make into a coherent whole. Make into a unit. Produce a new whole out of parts. Put together to make one. Reconstruct. Relate so as to produce a perfect whole. Syncretize. Systematize. Unite so as to produce a compound.

POLARIZATION. Antithesis. Balance between opposites. Complement. Contrapose. Contrast. Counteract. Countervail. Harmoniously oppose. Juxtaposed opposites. Mutually supplement. Opposites that neutralize. Supportive duality. Transmute through dualistic opposition.

OMEGALIZATION. Evolve into an absolute unity.

The eight principal ways of oneness are subdivided into twenty ways of oneness which may be identified as follows:

1. West annihilates East. $W \cdot \sim E$

2. East annihilates West. $E \cdot \sim W$

3. Mutual annihilation. $\sim E \cdot \sim W$

4. Both annihilated by a third. $X \cdot \sim E \cdot \sim W$

5. West assimilates East. $W \rightarrow \odot \!\!\!-\!\!\! E$

6. East assimilates West. $E \rightarrow \odot \!\!\!-\!\!\! W$

7. Both assimilated by a third. $E \!\!-\!\!\! \bigodot \!\!\!-\!\!\! W \;\; \leftarrow X$

8. West dominates East. $\dfrac{W}{E}$

9. East dominates West. $\dfrac{E}{W}$

10. Both dominated by a third. $\dfrac{X}{E \cdot W}$

11. Accommodation. $E\text{–}W$

12. Integration. WE

13. Synthesis between East and West. $E \rightarrow \bigcirc\!\!\bigcirc \leftarrow W$

14. Synthesis of East and West, West distorted. $W \rightarrow \bigcirc\!\!\!\bigcirc \leftarrow E$

15. Synthesis of East and West, East distorted. $E \rightarrow \bigcirc\!\!\!\bigcirc \leftarrow W$

16. Synthesis of East and West, both distorted.

17. Polarization, West diminished. $w \rightleftarrows E$

18. Polarization, East diminished. $W \rightleftarrows e$

19. Polarization, both diminished. $e \rightleftarrows w$

20. Omegalization: ○

1. The Ways of Annihilation.

The simplest way by which two antagonists can establish oneness is for one to destroy the other. This is the way of warfare and Christian missions. Julius Richter of the University of Berlin wrote in 1913, "Wherever missionary enterprise comes into contact with non-Christian religions it sets itself to oust them and to put Christianity in their place."[64] C. J. Shebbeare, Rector of Stanhope and Chaplain to the King, formerly Wilde Lecturer in Natural and Comparative Religion in Oxford University, wrote as the first sentence of his book *Christianity and Other Religions,* "The aim of the Christian missionary is to abolish all other religions of the world in favour of his own."[65] Shebbeare says that this aim cannot be justified unless it can be shown that Christianity is the "absolute religion," great regard for politeness, are shocked at this unseasonable proselytism as at something grossly vulgar."[81] They justify this high and controversial claim."[67] This is exactly what the author attempts to do in the work. Shebbeare, it should be noted, is an intelligent, informed person who seriously supports the view that Christianity should eliminate all other religions.

Pierre Teilhard de Chardin considered Christianity to be "the only possible religion,"[68] "the only factually possible religion,"[69] and "the only logically possible."[70] Therefore, he concluded that "we Christians must produce many more missionaries."[71]

Karl Barth offered a rationale for an attitude of destruction toward all non-Christian religions: "God has revealed Himself to man in Jesus Christ. What do we know from any other source about 'God,' the 'world' and 'Man,' and their mutual relations? We know absolutely nothing, and everything becomes confused myth and wild metaphysics as soon as we turn aside from the statement of that fact by which God Himself has confirmed, explained and laid down the relationship of God, the world and man, and God's ordinances."[72] Did Barth actually believe that the revelation in Jesus the Christ contains all that can be known about God, the world, and man? Did he think the Bible made all other sources of knowledge redundant? Such claims do Christianity great harm. They reflect badly on Barth's intelligence. Such extravagant remarks echo the earlier gasconades of John Knox: "What is in Asia? Ignorance of God. What is in Africa? Abnegation of the Veric Saviour, our Lord Jesus. What is in the Churches of the Grecianis? Mohamet and his false sect. What is in Rome? The greatest ydoll of all uthers, that man of syn."[73] One wonders why Knox did not also disparage the Irish, the English, the people of Glasgow, and the villagers on the outskirts of Edinburgh!

Emil Brunner made similar extravagant claims for Christianity. Although he admitted early in *The Mediator*, "No religion in the world, not even the most primitive, is without some elements of truth,"[74] he later added that there is a fundamental distinction between "general revelation" and "special revelation," between all forms of "popular religion" and the Christian religion. Only the Christian religion has "The Mediator." The Christian religion is based on "one single event," "one fact of revelation," an event "which took place once for all."[75] The German word *Einmaligkeit*, which Brunner used may be translated "oneness" or "once for all." The essential notion, says the translator, is "a unique moment in *time*." She adds that "unrepeatableness" is the real meaning.[76] Brunner contended that because of its *Einmaligkeit* Christianity and the non-Christian religions "confront each other in opposite camps; here there can be no reconciliation. Only one of these views can be true."[77] He added, "The religion of our classical writers, that of the poets as well as the philosophers, is essentially, not Christianity but this religion of general revelation, religion without a Mediator."[78] To be a Christian, he wrote, "means precisely to trust in the Mediator."[79] The relationship between Christianity and other religions is "irreconcilable, unbridgeable, fatal opposition."[80]

The Christian missionaries did not go to "the heathen" to learn from them but to convert them to Christian—and Western—ways of thinking and acting. One wonders how many of the missionaries realized, in the words of René Guénon that, "Orientals, who have all a great regard for politeness, are shocked at this unseasonable proselytism as at something grossly vulgar."[81] They did not know that in the minds of Orientals proselytism is "a proof of ignorance and incomprehension."[82]

Mahatma Gandhi had the Christian missionary in mind when he wrote that it is "the height of intolerance—and intolerance is a species of violence—to believe that your religion is superior to other religions and that you would be justified in wanting others to change to your faith."[83]

The missionary syndrome of "death to the enemy" was humorously revealed in an event in the life of Bertrand Russell. When he was erroneously reported to have died in China, a missionary journal published the following one-line obituary: "Missionaries may be pardoned for heaving a sigh of relief at the news of Mr. Bertrand Russell's death."[84] Less humorous is Radhakrishnan's report that when the African explorer, H. M. Stanley, inspected the original maxim gun, he observed, "What a splendid instrument for spreading Christianity and civilization among the savage races of Africa."[85]

Radhakrishnan, according to D. M. Datta, was motivated to spend twenty years in writing the two-volume work, Indian Philosophy, in order to counter the "harmful propaganda carried on not only by missionaries in India, but also by Indologists abroad and the latter's satellites in India."[86] Datta also says concerning Eastern Religions and Western Thought, "Its four hundred pages are packed with the sickening details of the political, cultural, and religious history of the world from the dawn of civilization."[87] Radhakrishnan closes that book with this paragraph: "Religions by propagating illusions such as the fear of hell, damnation, and arrogant assumptions of inviolable authority and excessive monopolies of the divine word and politics, by intoxicating whole peoples with dreams of their messianic missions, by engendering in them false memories, by keeping the old wounds open, by developing in them megalomania or persecution complex, destroy the sense of oneness with the world and divide humanity into narrow groups which are vain and ambitious, bitter and intolerant."[88] Radhakrishnan, speaking before the International Congress of World Fellowship of Faith in Tokyo on October 3, 1956, said, "We cannot have respect for another religion when all the time our attempt is to obliterate it."[89]

I do not choose to enter into an evaluation of Radhakrishnan's charges against Christianity other than to note that some Christian scholars disagree with him. For example, Hendrick Kraemer writes, "He [Radhakrishnan] misunderstands Christianity completely. . . . [He] manifests not only misunderstandings but a very strong dislike and aversion."[90] According to Stephen Neill, Radhakrishnan in his writings expresses "a dislike, amounting at times to a passionate hatred, of Christianity."[91]

Radhakrishnan and Tagore praised the elements of peace, good will, and nonmaterialism that they found in all religions and uniquely in Hinduism. Both despised the divine nature of sectarian religions. Radhakrishnan said, "Rabindranath's religious message is simple: Stick to religion. Let religions go."[92] Tagore in a long letter written on September 16, 1934 to Gilbert Murray condemned the "calumnies" of "sectarian religion."[93] In the same letter he wrote that "religion today as it exists in its prevalent institutionalized forms both in the West and in the East has failed in its function to control and guide the forces of humanity."[94]

In 1959 when I was in residence at Shantiniketan a

member of the community told me he admired Christianity but he hated "Churchianity." The most absurd example of sectarianism of which I am aware is a denomination named "The American Swedish Lutheran Church of France in India." A distinction between Christianity and Christendom is long overdue.

In an address before the All-India Oriental Conference at Annamalai University on December 26, 1955 Radhakrishnan said, "The world has bled and suffered from the disease of dogmatism, of conformity, of intolerance. People conscious of a mission to bring humanity to their own way of life, whether in religion or politics, have been aggressive towards other ways of life. The crusading spirit has spoiled the records of religions. . . . The tradition of opposition to one another must yield to co-operation."[95]

Joachim Wach agrees when Radhakrishnan states that "no doctrine becomes sounder, no truth truer, because it takes the aid of force,"[96] but he cannot accept Radhakrishnan's demand that Christians stop proselytism since, according to Wach's understanding of Christianity, "to surrender all attempts of inviting and winning others to the cause of Christ, would actually be to deny him."[97] Perhaps Wach should examine what is involved in "inviting and winning others to the cause of Christ." Usually it means to join in a Christian church with its specific dogma, structure, polity, sacraments, and tradition. Once, while in West Bengal, a Hindu friend told me a Methodist missionary lived nearby whom he regarded as the best Christian he knew. Later I visited the missionary. In the course of our conversation he remarked, "If there will be any stars in my crown, it will be because I have never asked a Hindu to become a Christian." Would Wach contend this missionary had denied the Christ?

William Ernest Hocking in *Living Religions and a World Faith* analyzes "three ways to a world faith": Radical displacement, Synthesis, Reconception. The first way, he says, is "the natural method of the missionary consciousness."[98] He refers to Karl Barth's advice that the missionary is not "to fraternize, nor accept the fellowship of fallen faiths . . . [and] in no circumstance is he to howl with the wolves."[99] Hocking comments, "The Barthian attempt to revive . . . exclusiveness is, with all its reinvigorating power, an evident failure."[100] He adds, "The religions of Asia are not wolves."[101]

Radhakrishnan writes that he was "the second son of Hindu parents, who were conventional in their religious outlook."[102] The atmosphere of the home was one in which "the unseen was a living reality."[103] He attended Christian schools for twelve years: Lutheran Mission High School (Tirupati) from 1896 to 1900, Voorhees' College (Vellore) from 1900 to 1904, and Madras Christian College from 1904 to 1908. He comments concerning those years, "My teachers in Christian missionary institutions cured me of this faith [faith in the unseen living reality] and restored for me the primordial situation in which all philosophy is born. They were teachers of philosophy, commentators, interpreters, apologists for the Christian way of thought and life, but were not in the strict sense of the term, seekers for truth. By their criticism of Indian thought they disturbed my faith and shook the traditional props on which I leaned. . . . A critical study of the Hindu religion was forced upon me."[104] His experience with Christian missionaries led him to conclude there is a need for a "new world society" with a "new world outlook."[105] This will involve "an abandonment of missionary enterprises."[106] We need "a basis for international understanding and co-operation."[107] "The main purpose of religious education" according to Radhakrishnan "is not to train others in our own way of thinking and living, not to substitute one form of belief for another, but to find out what others have been doing and help them to do it better."[108] Missionary motives, he says, "are derived from the conviction of the absolute superiority of our religion and of supreme contempt for other religions."[109] Such activities, if continued, "will become a prime factor in the spiritual impoverishment of the world."[110]

Louis Renou has pointed out that, whereas Radha-krishnan sometimes referred to "missionary religions" with the implication that Hinduism is not such, "The diffusion of Vaiṣṇavite and Śaivite ideas outside India is enough to show Hinduism, too, was a missionary reli-gion."[111] I find Renou's argument not very convincing. "Diffusion" is not what Christian missionaries do. The motto of the Student Volunteers in the early years of that movement was "The world for Christ in this generation." The aim of the Christian missionary was and is that "every knee shall bow" and "every tongue confess." This is not "diffusion." The Ārya Samāj is one Hindu cult which has marched to that tune.

Radhakrishnan is silent about a very interesting con-flict within Indian philosophy: the continuing conflict between the Advaitins and the Viśiṣṭādvaitins. Rāmānuja referred to the followers of Śaṅkara as "our adversary."[112] He said of their writings, "All this reasoning . . . is entirely spun out of your fancy."[113] And, after warming to his argument, he made this indictment of Śaṅkara's interpre-tation of *The Vedānta Sūtras*: "This entire theory rests on a fictitious foundation of altogether hollow and vicious arguments, incapable of being stated in definite logical alternatives, and devised by men who are destitute of those particular qualities which cause individuals to be chosen by the Supreme Person revealed in the Upaniṣads; whose intellects are darkened by the impres-sion of beginningless evil; and who thus have no insight into the nature of words and sentences, into the real pur-port conveyed by them, and into the procedure of sound argumentation, with all its methods depending on perception and the other means of knowledge—assisted by sound reasoning—have an insight into the true nature of things."[114] This inaugurates an attack on the followers of Śaṅkara which in the Thibaut translation runs from page 39 to page 156! How Radhakrishnan could have closed his mind to this effort to refute, convert, and annihilate the Śaṅkarites is difficult to understand. This is why I conclude that Radhakrishnan was often an apologistic philosopher—if there is such! It is not without interest or significance to note that Radhakrishnan devotes 213 pages to Śaṅkara in his *Indian Philosophy* and only 63 pages to Rāmānuja.

Radhakrishnan writes that if the different religions wish to terminate conflict "they must develop a spirit of comprehension which will break down prejudice and misunderstanding and bind them together as varied expressions of a single truth."[115] He claims that this is the spirit of which has "characterized the development of Hinduism."[116] The spirit of comprehension, he says, "has not been interrupted for nearly fifty centuries."[117] I suggest that Radhakrishnan might have looked again at Kautilya's *Arthaśāstra*, a Hindu handbook written about 300 B.C.E. This is a guide for rulers with explicit directions for crafty intrigue, deception of the ruled, techniques for injuring enemies, ways of destroying traitors, methods of avoiding peoples' revolution, directions for use of spies, and recipes for poisoning enemies. Torture is outlined in detail as a way to implement the general principle that those believed to be guilty should be tortured. According to *The Oxford History of India* "The theory of politics expounded in the *Arthaśāstra* is substantially identical with that of *The Prince*."[118]

Radhakrishnan also does not note that in 261 B.C.E. King Aśoka, before becoming a Buddhist, waged war on Kalinga. In that war, according to Rock Edict No. 13, 150,000 persons were carried away captive, 100,000 were slain, and many times that number died. Radhakrishnan does not notice that Buddhism survives in the world today because Aśoka and Tissa, his successor, sent Buddhist missionaries to Asia, to Africa, and perhaps to Europe. One of the most successful of these missions was the one led by Malinda, said to have been either Aśoka's son or his younger brother. Today there are about 100,000 Buddhists in India. They live largely along the borders of Nepal and Tibet. The extermination of Buddhism in India—including the great University of Nalanda—cannot be laid solely on the Muslims!

Another curious inconsistency in the basic pacifism of Radhakrishnan is to be found in his study of the *Bhagavad Gītā*. Radhakrishnan, rather than condemning Kṛṣṇa's advice to Arjuna to fight, justifies the war: "War happens to be the occasion which the teacher uses to indicate the spirit in which all work including warfare will have to be performed."[119]

There are four ways of oneness by annihilation. The West can annihilate the East, or the East can annihilate the West, physically, intellectually, economically, politically, culturally, or in any other conceivable, or as yet unconceived, manner. A third possibility is that another people, for example, Africans, South Americans, or Australians, might eliminate both East and West from their current positions as centers of authority and significance. A fourth possibility is the horrible thought that through nuclear weapons or through the destruction of life support systems the East and/or the West might destroy the entire human race. That would result in the oneness of total annihilation.

2. The Ways of Assimilation.

Assimilation as a way to oneness is similar to annihilation. Annihilation is reduction to nonexistence. Assimilation is reduction to dependent existence. That which has been assimilated has lost its independent status but retains some of its original nature, although in a transmogrified condition. When sugar has dissolved in a cup of coffee, it no longer possesses a granulated condition, but its sweetness remains. The charge made by the Nazis in Germany during the years before World War II was that the Jews did not assimilate into the populace. They retained too much Jewishness. The problems of cultural assimilation are numerous. What elements must be changed? How much alteration is required? How can absorption be measured? How much of the process of assimilation can or should be voluntary? Can either side initiate the assimilation process?

There are three ways of assimilation. The West may assimilate the East. The East may assimilate the West. Both East and West may be assimilated by a third culture.

Hinduism has a reputation for absorbing diverse ways of thinking and acting. Radhakrishnan praises the willingness of Hindus to consume and digest a wide variety of ideas and practices: "The strength of Hinduism is its power of assimilation."[120] "The Vedic religion . . . absorbed, embodied, and preserved the types of rituals of older cults."[121] It "adapted them to its own requirements."[122] "Hinduism absorbs everything that enters into it, magic or animinism, and raises it to a higher good."[123] P. T. Raju writes, "As a religion, Hinduism is said to be all-absorbing; its assimilative power is stupendous."[124] Jawarhalal Nehru once said that India's borrowing is like a palimpsest, a manuscript on which layer after layer of writing has been done without completely obliterating the previous writing. Richard Lannoy refers to "the Indian way of borrowing while conserving, of juxtaposing the new and the old in hierarchical relations."[125]

A critic might contend that Hinduism's propensity toward assimilation is evidence of the undeveloped character of the religion, of insecurity, of primitiveness, of a need for hierarchical authority. *Hinduism*, the critic might argue, does not denote a religion but a wide variety of modes of thought and forms of behavior which have never been properly sorted out and related to each other.

René Guénon, on the other hand, praises the Hindu tendency to assimilate. Assimilation is propaedeutic to interpretation: "the first condition for the correct interpretation of any doctrine is to make an effort to assimilate it by placing oneself as far as possible at the viewpoint of those who conceived it."[126] This aspect of Hinduism made a favorable impression upon me when during my first year in India I was invited to help plan and participate in a Christmas worship service in a Hindu temple which honored Jesus as an *avatāra* (earthly manifestation) of divinity. Also during that year a Jesuit told me he had become an Indian citizen, fearing that his superiors in Belgium would cancel his passport if they learned how much he had come to admire the kindly assimilative traits of Hinduism. Bishop John A. T. Robinson in *Truth is Two-Eyed*[127] reports his surprise upon discovering that Indian Christians had developed insights into Christianity that had been overlooked in the West.

Radhakrishnan in that curious fluid logic, for which he is both praised and condemned, claimed that although the culture of India has assimilated much it has remained the same. He writes in *The Brahma Sūtra*, "The culture of India has changed a great deal and yet has remained the same for over three millennia. Fresh springs bubble up, fresh streams cut their own channels through the landscape, but sooner or later each rivulet, each stream merges into one of the great rivers which has been nourishing the Indian soil for centuries."[128]

Radhakrishnan argues that, because of India's willingness to absorb foreigners, there are fewer outcaste peoples in India than there would be had any culture other than the Hindu been dominant. However, we should keep in mind that an argument that history would have been different if events that happened had not happened is an amazing argument! His words are: "Outsiders have been steadily flowing into the Hindu fold, and the religion has been able to absorb and inspire heterogeneous peoples with elements of the higher life. But for this civilizing work India would have had, instead of fifty million untouchables, five times that number. This work has ceased to be effective since the loss of political freedom by the Hindus. It was then that Hindu society became fixed in a conservatism and left outside its pale a considerable part of the population of India, which has been the field of exploitation by the non-Hindu religions."[129] There are many things to say about this section of the book. First, the idea of exonerating Hinduism from creating untouchability so appealed to him that he repeated the statement: "If the work of civilizing the backward classes had not been undertaken and carried on with zeal and success by the ancient Indians, we would have had not merely fifty millions of these 'depressed' classes, but a much larger number. When the outside invaders came into the country, the Hindu felt nervous, and, as a sheer act of self-preservation, stereotyped the existing divisions, and some tribes were left outside the pale of the caste order."[130] This repetition may be attributed not to loss of memory but to the fact that much of his published materials was originally lectures or addresses to various audiences. Second, note his tendency to blame untouchability on the Muslims and the British. They made us nervous! They forced us to preserve ourselves by keeping some tribes outside the caste system! "The caste rules were not rigid until the advent of the Mohammedans into India."[131] He carefully avoids mentioning that the Christian missionaries directed much of their efforts to alleviating the conditions of the untouchables, and that many of the untouchables became Christians in order to escape the caste system. In the third place his reference to "free India" is puzzling: "It is not remembered that a free India rendered them [the untouchables] much greater service than what other free countries even in recent times have done for their backward classes."[132] I wonder how much credit modern India can claim for the Gandhian efforts to help the Harijans. I am not aware of any methodology for comparing the eleemosynary efforts of the ancient Hindus with respect to the backward classes with similar efforts in Africa, America, Australia, the Philippine Islands, and elsewhere where this problem exists.

Shanti Nath Gupta has pointed to a very significant assimilation within Hinduism. This is the incorporation of the secondary values (artha, kāma, and dharma, that is, material wealth, erotic pleasures, and moral duties) within the primary values (mokṣa and Brahman, that is, salvation and Absolute Unity). This integration, he says, is a major achievement of the Vedānta of Śaṅkara. According to this interpretation of the Vedānta, writes the author, "the transcendental is not the negation of the empirical but in a sense its consummation and culmination so that empirical values are the reflections or the imperfect and limited expressions of the fullness of the transcendental, e.g., empirical pleasure (kāma) is nothing but a limited and partial manifestation of the infinite bliss (ānanda). The limitations here are due to the defects and inadequate psychic modes which the lower manifestations have to pass through. Hence, there is no antagonism between the higher and the lower values: they can be interrelated and integrated into one system in which the distinctions on axiological and ontological grounds remain valid for their hierarchical gradation into the higher and lower."[133]

William S. Haas wrote in 1956 that the East is faced with "the crucial problem of assimilating a civilization which is contrary to its own."[134] I suspect that Haas suffered as many did at that time from a stereotyped view of the East. Western peoples in the decades following World War II might well have paid more attention to the pluralities of Eastern cultures. Haas did correctly note, "The very delimitation of the term East seems to have lost its meaning amid recent happenings."[135] If this observation was appropriate in 1956, how much more appropriate is it thirty years later!

Haas in the volume calls attention to the fact that, while the West has produced many philosophical systems, it has been incapable of producing a great religion. Instead it had adopted a Near Eastern religion, and recreated it to fit Western institutions, ideals, and ways of knowing. The result is insecurity and uncertainty beyond that experienced by any Eastern people. Haas's words are: "Prolific mainly in philosophical systems and incapable of producing a great religion the Western mind bordered on religion but it had to rely on another power to open the door to that inner sanctum. This inability to create a religion, and the adoption of a foreign one coupled with the gigantic effort to assimilate it by recreating it are the deeply rooted causes of this deep uncertainty in the West. Such doubt could emanate only from the depth of the spirit and it is unknown to the East."[136] Especially since the eighteenth century, Haas adds, Western civilization has become increasingly enigmatic with regard to itself. It is "doubtful as to its essence and value—uneasy as to road and objective."[137]

According to Louis Renou, "In the field of speculation, the writings and teachings of Radhakrishnan and Aurobindo Ghose may be considered as attempts to modernize Hinduism and to utilize its living power by adapting it to the needs of minds accustomed to Western theology and philosophy. Radhakrishnan eradicates from Indian forms all features that are peculiar to them, and builds them into a symbolism that can be adapted to any form of religion. Aurobindo preaches a new syncretism based on a reinterpretation of the religious manifestations of India, from the Vedānta to Tantrism."[138]

Mahatma Gandhi believed that borrowing between India and the West should be mutual—with India offering a bit more in the trade: "I would gladly borrow from the West when I can return the amount with decent interest."[139] K. C. Bhattacharyya put this much more bluntly: "A synthesis of our ideals with Western ideals is not demanded in every case. Where it is demanded, the foreign ideal is to be assimilated to our ideal and not the other way."[140] Guénon agrees that the East has more to offer in assimilation. He says that the West must "approach the East, since it is the West that has gone astray."[141] Yet the process will not be easy, because, as he says, "The Orientals are not in the least bent on absorbing the West."[142] Haas disagrees. At least he thinks the East can absorb the West without loss of Eastern values: "Representative Easterners often express the view that Western civilization can be successfully assimilated without affecting the core of the Eastern essence."[143] Would Haas have the same view were he writing about Japan today? Japan has assimilated so many Western values and technical skills since 1945 that one can ask how much of the traditional Japan remains. The Japanese tourists in

Europe and North America do not look like Nanki-Poo or Yum-Yum!

Nirad C. Chaudhuri chastises Westerners who try to assimilate elements of Hinduism. He writes," After losing the mental stability and spiritual confidence which came from Christianity many people in the West are coming round to think that they can find a substitute in certain things in Hinduism, e.g., Yoga. Also, they have undermined repose and happiness in their daily life by a manner of conducting it which is almost devoid of sanity, and are taking recourse to the same Yoga and also to Vaishnavism, which is no better than taking drugs."[144] Chaudhuri errs in not recognizing there are some Westerners who are able to assimilate part of Oriental thought and practice into their lives without loss of their own traditional values. Not all who seek light from the East become pseudo-Orientals—or even quasi-Orientals.

Chaudhuri's implication that yoga, which admittedly originated within Hinduism, cannot be assimilated by Westerners needs to be challenged. Many Westerners have profited by introducing *hatha yoga* into their daily lives. Jean Décharet, a Roman Catholic priest, utilizes yoga in his meditations. In his book, *Christian Yoga*, he upbraids "Indianizers," who adopt the superficial aspects of Indian culture.[145] He writes, "The essential point is to understand thoroughly and to admit that it is not a question of turning a given form of Yoga into something Christian, but of bringing into the service of Christianity and of the Christian life (especially when this is given up to contemplation) the undoubted benefits arising from yogic disciplines. Everything in Yoga, therefore, that promotes dialogue, the basic Christian dialogue, may be boldly considered as fit for adaptation."[146] Décharet's example is a fine application of Gandhi's admonition to leave one's windows open to all cultures without being blown off one's feet.

3. The Ways of Domination.

Annihilation is the way of Christian missions. Assimilation is the way of sugar in coffee. Domination is the way of the brute beast—the bull moose among the cows, the wolf in the pack, and the songbird establishing territory in the woods. Domination is also a way to oneness among humans in communities and among nations. Radhakrishnan has observed, "There are two ways in which the realization of world-unity can be brought about, world-domination and world-commonwealth."[147]

The Roman Empire was based on domination. Rome brought peace and order to the warring tribes of Europe through military strength. When the Roman legions reached a limit of domination, they built a wall, for example, Hadrian's Wall, indicating the boundary of *Pax Romana*. Ancient Greeks sought unity of mind and body— a sound mind in a healthy body. Ancient Romans sought unity of society, law, culture. Christianity with roots in Hebraism was nurtured and modified by both Greece and Rome.

Christianity during the first three hundred years of its existence sought to survive in the Roman world. During the second three hundred years Christianity learned the techniques of domination. The attitude of the Roman government toward the new cult was at first one of tolerant indifference. During a few brief periods the Christian community was used as a scapegoat by besieged emperors.

A change took place early in the fourth century. That change is associated in fact and legend with Constantine I, who came to be known as Constantine the Great.

Constantine, the Caesar (junior emperor) of Gaul and Britain, sought to challenge Maxentius's rule of Italy, Africa, and Spain. Shortly before the crucial battle at Milvian Bridge, which took place on October 28, 312, Constantine is reported to have seen a cross of light in the sky and over the cross the legend *En toútō víka* (Conquer by this). Constantine, after defeating Maxentius, erected in Rome a statue of himself, cross in hand, and on the cross the following: "By this salutary sign, the true proof of bravery, I have saved and freed your city from the yoke of the tyrant."[148]

Constantine, assuming he had been chosen for rule by the god of the Christians, sought instruction in the Christian faith and added Christian symbols to Roman life. A cross was placed on certain coins, and the Christian monogram ☧ was placed on his troops' shields. One legend is that he put nails from the original cross on the bridle of his horse in fulfillment of the prophecy of *Zechariah* 14:20 "On the bridles, Holiness to the Lord." By 321 the non-Christian soldiers in the Roman army were required to assemble each Sunday morning to recite in unison: "We acknowledge thee the only God. We own thee as our King and implore thy succor. By thy favor have we gotten victory; through thee we are mightier than our enemies. We render thanks for thy past benefits and trust thee for future blessings; together we pray thee and beseech thee long to preserve us safe and triumphant, our emperor, Constantine and his pious sons."[149]

The act of most significance to the Christians was the Edict of Milan (313) signed by both Constantine as western emperor and Licinius as eastern emperor. The crucial statement in the Edict is the following: "Perceiving long ago that religious liberty ought not to be denied, but that it ought to be granted to the judgment and desire of each individual to perform his religious duties according to his own free choice, we had given orders that every man, Christian as well as others should preserve the faith of his own sect and religion . . . to grant both to the Christians and to all men freedom to follow the religion which they choose."[150] The Christians rejoined by conferring upon Constantine encomiums such as "The New Moses" and "The Thirteenth Apostle." Christendom began to learn the arts and crafts of domination. The chief lesson a persecuted people learn is how to persecute.

Constantine moved the seat of empire from Rome. In 326 the cornerstone of Constantinople was laid, and on May 11, 330 the city was dedicated to the Blessed Virgin. The new location of the seat of power may have been part of Constantine's plan to change the quasi-constitutional monarchy into political absolutism (sometimes called the "Dominate"). In religious matters Constantine became the *pontifex maximus*. His hope was that the Christian Church would become an instrument of political power. What he did not foresee was that a powerful church would become the most determined opponent of despotic civil authority.

Perhaps Constantine's moving of the center of empire from Rome to Constantinople was an effort to move Christianity eastward. This was the direction Paul and Silas wished to move. But they were "forbidden." *The Acts of the Apostles* records they "were forbidden of the Holy Ghost to preach the word in Asia."[151] If this was the intention of Constantine, he was unsuccessful. He was unable to arrest the Western captivity of the Christian Church. John A. T. Robinson writes, "We think of Christianity now as being a Western religion, but this is only because it became that through men who took great risks in theology, spirituality and art, that we might know through the medium of our own cultural conditioning the wonderful works of God."[152] Robinson adds that, although "this cultural conditioning which has given us marvellous stories and shaped so rich a worth, intellectually, devotionally, architecturally, musically, and many other ways," it has become a "constriction."[153] Robinson happily announces, "In our one world men and women are turning East because they sense how one-eyed we in the West have become. And instinctively they recognize that no other country in the third world is so rich in spiritual resources as India and the places that India has influenced."[154] This Anglican bishop discovered, however, that many Christians prefer to remain "one-eyed" and that his Church prefers that its priests not be prophets!

Constantine, taking as his dictum "Whatever is determined in the holy assembly of the bishops is to regarded as indicative of the divine will,"[155] formulated laws favorable to Christianity. A list of some of the laws formulated by Constantine and his successors through Valentinian III, that is, from 313 to 527, illustrates the shift in the Roman attitude to Christianity and demonstrates the Christian Church's method of achieving oneness by domination:

> Clergy exempted from public duties. (313)
> Churches freed from *annona* and *tributum*. (313)
> Manumission in churches made legal. (316)
> Law disqualifying childless from inheritances changed.
>   (Probably so as not to disqualify celibate priests.) (320)
> Wills in favor of the Church permitted. (321)
> Sunday raised to the rank of the old pagan holidays
>   (*feriae*) by suspending work of courts and of city
>   population, although allowing agricultural work to be
>   done on Sunday. (321)
> Pagan temples closed. (346)
> Worshippers of idols punishable by death. (356)
> Divination forbidden. (357)
> Magic forbidden. (358)
> Astrology forbidden. (370)
> Right to bequeath or inherit property denied apostates.
>   (383)
> Visits to pagan shrines prohibited. (391)
> Paganism outlawed. (392)
> Pagan holidays abolished. (395)
> Rural temples to be destroyed. (399)
> Pagan temples appropriated by the Church. (408)
> Pagans banned from military and civil offices. (416)
> All pagan practices prohibited. (472)
> Property of pagans confiscated. (527)[156]

The flavor of these laws is indicated by a line from a law of Valentinian and Marcian dated November 12, 451 forbidding temple sacrifices: "Whoever, contrary to this order of our serenity and the commands of the most hallowed ancient decrees, seeks to make such sacrifices, shall be charged by due course of law with his shameful crime in open court, and upon conviction shall undergo the confiscation of all his property and the penalty of death."[157]

Christian domination in the twelfth and thirteenth centuries took the form of eight military expeditions to the East in an effort to free the so-called Holy Places from Muslim rule. The Crusades were neither the first nor the last effort to advance the gospel of the Prince of Peace by warfare. A student of the Crusades has evaluated them in this manner: "In the long sequence of interaction and fusion between Orient and Occident out of which our civilization has grown, the Crusades were a tragic and destructive episode. . . . High ideals were besmirched by cruelty and greed, enterprise and endurance by a blind and narrow self-righteousness; and the Holy War itself was nothing more than a long act of intolerance in the name of God."[158]

I find it hard to believe that intelligent and informed Christians can still defend a dominating Christianity. Yet this is the case. For example, J. V. Langmead Casserley, a Christian theologian, writes that "a Christ who would be quite happy in a pantheon, His image tolerantly rubbing shoulders with those of Buddha or Confucius, Mahomet and perhaps Gandhi" would be a Christ "who would never have inspired the martyrs or given the early Church the will to survive the Roman persecution."[159] To affirm that Jesus the Christ would not care to associate with Gandhi, one of the most Christlike men of this century, is very strange. And how does Casserley know that a tolerant Christ would not inspire martyrdom? Does he not realize that faithfulness to an ideology in the face of persecution is found in Judaism, Zoroastrianism, Islam, Buddhism, Hinduism, Sikhism, Jainism, Confucianism, Taoism, and Shinto as well as in Christianity? Has he forgotten the millions of men and women who have died in defense of their nations? When will Christians realize that Christianity is not the only ideal which inspires total dedication? Never as long as Christian theologians blazon, "There has been most emphatically no advance beyond Christianity in any field whatsoever."[160]

Domination has disfigured Christianity both in the West and in the East. R. H. S. Boyd notes that the general policy of the Portuguese Roman Catholic missionary movement in India in the sixteenth century was "to use the power of the sword to promote the expansion of the Church."[161] The native converts thus assumed physical force was the proper mode of evangelism. There is a record of a Chinese *tuchum* (warlord) who baptized his soldiers with water sprayed from a fire hose and marched them into battle to the tune "Onward Christian Soldiers."[162]

Teilhard de Chardin, the Jesuit who suffered by reason of Vatican prohibitions, could still write that he hoped to discover "a Christ who is not only a model of good conduct and of 'humanity'; but the superhuman Being who, for ever in formation in the heart of the world, possesses a being capable of bending all, and assembling all, by vital *domination*."[163] Teilhard's approval of domination is puzzling when one reads that in 1925 he was forced by the Church at Rome to cease spreading his "gospel of research" on the evolution of man and to submit to papal authority concerning the literal truth of the creation stories of *Genesis*. (By coincidence 1925 was also the year in which the State of Tennessee limited the right to use human intelligence with respect to the theory of human origins.) On February 12, 1929 Teilhard wrote, "The time has come for us to save Christ from the clerics, in order to save the World,"[164] but he could not follow through with a forthright confrontation against the domination of the Holy Office in Rome. He died in 1955, a faithful but frustrated son of the Church.

Radhakrishnan despised the establishment of oneness by means of domination. He was very sensitive to this tendency in the Christian Church. He said rather coyly in an address on May 29, 1955 before the Union for the Study of the Great Religions (India Branch): "This ambition to make disciples of all nations is not the invention of the Communists."[165] The West, he said, wants "to subjugate everything."[166] This dominating spirit he found especially exasperating in missionary religions: "Each claims with absolute sincerity that it alone is the true light while others are will-'o-the-wisps that blind us to the truth and lure us away from it. When it attempts to be a little more understanding, it affirms that the light of its religion is to that of others as the sun is to the stars, and the mirror lights may be tolerated so long as they accept their position of subordination."[167]

Radhakrishnan praised India for its absence of a spirit of domination: "Universalism has been innate in the Indian character."[168] He added that "it has assumed a high, pure and noble form and so has won for us the sympathy and admiration of the world. It never took the shape of an ambition for world domination. It has shaped itself as world sympathy, understanding, open-mindedness and so has contributed to the enrichment of the world."[169] Yet sometimes he admitted to Hindu domination. For example, in The Hindu View of Life he writes, "In its southward march the Aryan culture got in touch with the Dravidian and ultimately dominated it."[170]

Even though Radhakrishnan often returns to the theme that India and Hinduism are not dominating, he affirms another strange form of domination. This is the insistence that India is the guru to the West. The West, he advises, ought to submit itself to what India has to teach. Robert Browning calls attention to Radhakrishnan's view that India is the dominating physician. The West is an ill patient, and India is the physician hovering over the helpless object of healing medication and therapy.[171]

The most flagrant example of domination in India is surely the practice of untouchability. Radhakrishnan belatedly and rather mildly condemns untouchability in Religion and Society (1947). One does not find in Radhakrishnan a stinging rebuke of untouchability such as Gandhi's attack: "I regard untouchability as the greatest blot on Hinduism. . . . To say that Hinduism, which once discovered the Universality of Spirit, the Oneness of Soul, the doctrine of One in All and All in one, sanctions Untouchability of any sort, is to deny and undo the very Truth, meditated upon and realized by the great Seers."[172]

Western people, who are shocked by the remnants of untouchability in India, must not forget their own history. Columbus is reported to have said upon first seeing the peaceful Arawak people, "They would make wonderful servants. With forty men we could subjugate them all." The European invaders of the "empty continent," who called themselves "settlers" and "colonists," acted for the most part on the principle that the only good Indian is a dead Indian. To this day the descendants of these native Americans are largely confined to reservations.

Domination is a persistent theme in human history: males over females, lords over vassals, masters over slaves, employers over employees, age over youth. Domination is a way to oneness—until the dominated rebel.

William S. Haas in *The Destiny of the Mind: East and West* argues that, unless significant epistemological changes are made in the East, unity of East and West will be achieved by Western domination. This, he says, is because Western knowing is a form of grasping, whereas Eastern knowing is a form of being. To have knowledge in the West means to have seized the object of knowledge, to have made it subordinate to the wishes of the knower. "I know X" means "I have X under my control." To have knowledge in the East means to have brought about changes in the subject. "I know X" means "I have changed from being a non-knower-of-X to being a knower-of-X." This may be a far too facile summary of Eastern and Western forms of knowing, but it is the case that Western knowing tends to be object oriented, and Eastern knowing tends to be subject oriented. There is the possibility that when the Western knower selects as the epistemological object the Eastern knower, and when the Eastern knower stresses himself or herself as knower, the dominated will be the Eastern person. Haas concludes, "Although the Eastern structure and thereby its creations as well as its forms of life, are in principle equally capable of world-wide diffusion, the East cannot hope to compete in point of expansion with the objectifying mind of the

West. For the Eastern mind and civilization necessarily lack the dynamic which is the monopoly of the objectifying mind. Were the West not what it is, Eastern civilization in a slow and static process would no doubt be on the way to world civilization."[173]

4. The Ways of Accommodation.

The annihilator says, "There will be oneness, after I have destroyed you." The assimilator says, "There will be oneness, after I have absorbed you." The dominator says, "There will be oneness, after I have established supremacy over you." The accommodator says, "There will be oneness after we have acknowledged each other." Annihilation, assimilation, and domination are imposed by one on the other. The oneness of accommodation is a negotiated oneness. No one ever imposed accommodation on another.

Accommodation is a delicate, precarious, fragile form of oneness. The list of near-synonyms indicates that *accommodation* designates a wide variety of relations ranging from mere recognition of the existence of another to cooperation with another in order to realize ideal goals. The common denominator of the ways of accommodation is an attitude of tolerance.

When comparative philosophy was first presented in the West by Paul Masson-Oursel, it was regarded as a form of accommodation. Analogy, wrote Masson-Oursel, will be the "guiding principle." He defined analogy as "reasoning in accordance with what in mathematics is called a proportion, that is to say, the equality of two ratios;—A is to B as Y is to Z."[174] He illustrated this by pointing out that Socrates is to Greek Sophism as Confucius is to Chinese Sophism.[175]

Radhakrishnan was an accommodator. He was once described by one who knew him well as "a liaison officer between East and West."[176] *Liaison officer* is a military term to denote a person appointed to maintain contact between units in order to ensure concerted action. Perhaps it is a fitting designation of Radhakrishnan's life and work. He sought to help Eastern and Western philosophers recognize the existence of each other, acknowledge the validity of each others' work in the philosophical enterprises, appreciate each others' assumptions, methods, and conclusions, and grow in willingness to work toward common goals.

Whatever may be the final evaluation of the life and work of Radhakrishnan, he is remembered as a pioneer in East-West understanding. "No one has done more than Radhakrishnan to interpret East and West to each other," wrote William Ralph Inge.[177] Radhakrishnan, rather than founding a new system of thought, set as his self-appointed task, according to P. T. Raju, grasping "the spirit of Eastern and Western thought" in order that he might present Indian philosophy in terms of "the ideology of the West."[178] Raju might have added that he also presented Indian philosophy beautifully in a Western language.

Radhakrishnan's writings have the flavor of *samanvaya* (reconciliation). It was his iterant claim that tolerance is the hallmark of Indian culture. "From the time the Aryans met the peoples of a lower grade of civilization, they devised ways and means by which the different portions of the population could develop in social, spiritual directions. The Aryans even accepted a non-Aryan representative of the 'black' peoples—Krishna, and made him deliver the message of the fatherhood of God and the brotherhood of man. Krishna's conduct scandalized society and provoked the Vedic gods of Indra and Brahmā. Today the Aryan worshippers of these gods look upon Krishna as an avatar of God."[179]

Radhakrishnan boasts that the tolerance Hinduism has shown to other faiths has resulted in Hinduism becoming "a mosaic of almost all types and stages of religious aspiration and endeavor. It has adapted itself with infinite grace to every human need and it has not shrunk from the acceptance of every aspect of God conceived by man, and yet preserved its unity by interpreting the different historical forms as modes, emanations, or aspects of the Supreme."[180] The resulting pluralism is "the homage which the finite mind pays to the inexhaustibility of the Infinite,"[181] adds Radhakrishnan, in a sentence which sounds rather poetic, but which makes little sense to me. In the same vein he wrote, "All religions she [India] welcomed, since she realized from the cloudy heights of contemplation that the spiritual landscape at the hill-top is the same, though the pathways from the valley are different."[182] The Hindu attitude, he continues, is "one of positive fellowship, not negative tolerance."[183] "The Hindu welcomes even the atheist into his field."[184]

Yet, asserts Radhakrishnan, "Hinduism does not mistake tolerance for indifference. It affirms that while all revelations refer to reality, they are not equally true to it."[185] Unfortunately he did not develop the conception of the inequalities of interpretation of śruti. A statement— and an elaboration—of the differences of Hindu sects would have been a more balanced presentation. The distinctions of varṇa (caste), jāti (vocation), gotra (lineage), marriage restrictions, diet restrictions, social customs, and religious preferences should not be ignored. I recall that the chairman of the department of philosophy in one of India's major universities would not eat lunch with me as my presence was polluting!

Radhakrishnan makes five statements concerning tolerance in The Hindu View of Life which I find puzzling: (1) "In the name of tolerance we [Hindus] have carefully protected superstitious rites and customs."[186] (I am not sure that this was done "in the name of tolerance." I doubt that the plurality of rites and customs in Hinduism was ever allowed in the name of tolerance. Maybe diversity was allowed because there were not sufficient controls to legislate uniformity.) (2) "The more religious we [Hindus] grow the more tolerant of diversity we become."[187] (How does one measure degrees of religiosity?) (3) "The Hindu thinker readily admits other points of view than his own and considers them to be just as worthy of attention."[188] (This broad generalization is not true. Anyone who has had contact with Hindu philosophers in conferences in India and outside of India knows very well that these men and women argue for position as do Western philosophers.) (4) "The Hindus took the gods of even the savage and the uncivilized and set them on equal thrones to his own."[189] (This is a very loose interpretation of the Hindu practice of *iṣṭadevatā* [chosen deity]. Radhakrishnan always had great admiration for Rabindranath Tagore. Yet, if this is Radhakrishnan's conception of Hinduism, Tagore as member of the Brāhmo Samāj was not a Hindu, since the Brāhmo Samāj rejected any god that was worshipped with images.) (5) Hinduism "is wholly free from the strange obsessions of the Semitic faiths," the view "that the acceptance of a particular religious metaphysics is necessary for salvation and non-acceptance thereof is a heinous sin meriting eternal punishment in hell."[190] (This criticism misfires. Orthodoxy is the "obsession" of Christianity. The Semitic "obsession" is orthopraxy. Also, Radhakrishnan does not take sufficiently into account the fact that there have been changes in the Christian attitude toward right belief. For example, the Tolerance Act of 1689 was an important act. G. M. Trevelyan says of this Act: "After a thousand years, religion was at length released from the obligation to practice cruelty on principle, by the admission that it is the incorrigible nature of man to hold different opinions on speculative subjects."[191])

Sometimes Radhakrishnan contrasts Hindu tolerance with American diplomacy. For example, he writes, "Hindu thought never developed a Monroe doctrine in matters of culture. Even in the ancient times when India grew enough spiritual food to satisfy her own people, there is no recorded age when she was not ready and eager to appreciate the products of other people's imagination."[192] Radhakrishnan was apologetic about Gandhi's movement of resistance and non-cooperation with the British: "The non-cooperation with Western culture is a passing episode due to unnatural circumstances."[193] He believed that when the "unnatural circumstances" ceased India would adopt many of the ideas of Western culture, and this, he stated, would be "only a repetition of parallel processes which happened a number of times in the history of Indian thought."[194]

Radhakrishnan says in *Eastern Religions and Western Thought* that tolerance saved the Hindus from "spiritual snobbery."[195] He had in mind the snobberies found in Christianity, Islam, and Judaism. He should have noted that people in various cultures are snobbish about different things. He could be reminded that, whereas anyone can enter any part of a Christian Church, in a Hindu temple non-Hindus are forbidden to enter the *garbha-grha* (womb house). Dining restrictions, marriage regulations, matters of physical proximity, and even visibility are some of the many snobberies of Hinduism. It would be most interesting to have heard Radhakrishnan's explanation of how he happened to marry his first cousin! His persistent affirmation of Hindu tolerance finally wears very thin. I fear it is a case of repeating an idea so often that the speaker thinks it irrefutable.

N. Subrahmanian's "The Hindu Tripod" is an antidote worth careful consideration. J. Duncan M. Derrett of the University of London, in the foreword to the volume containing this essay, praises the author for "the total absence of that Victorian 'mealy-mouthed' tone which is still a characteristic of well-bred Indian comment on Indian affairs designed for foreign as well as home consumption."[196] Subrahamanian says, "Normal Hindu reaction to exotic cultural influences is to ignore them; if that negative attitude was not sufficient for the purposes of warding off that influence the positive one of minimal adjustment to ease social frictions would be adopted while taking care to screen off from vulgar and alien gaze the inner and esoteric areas of socio-religious life."[197] Subrahmanian mentions two areas where compromise is impossible: matrimony and interdining. He adds, "With great reluctance Hindu orthodoxy tolerates non-Hindu ways of life when they impinge on it, providing its basic principles regarding caste and family are not seriously questioned."[198] The famous toleration of Aśoka, adds Subrahmanian, "started after his conversion to the Buddhist faith."[199] And to illustrate his argument Subrahamanian offers the following: "Pushyamitra, a Brahminical general, assassinated his Buddhist king; a Pallava monarch who while he was a Jaina persecuted the Śaivas and when he became a Śaivite persecuted the Jainas; the Gauda king Sansanka uprooted the sacred Bodhi tree of the Buddhists probably as a counter measure to Harsha's partiality to the Mahayanists; the Saiva Chola drove the greatest Vaishnava Acharya out of his realm; the Christian missionaries in the Tamil country were persecuted by the princes of the Setupati."[200] Subrahamanian observes that "tolerance was not an invariable rule but would be practised if possible and given up if necessary and both courses were expedient."[201] "Tolerance, in the Hindu context," he writes, "is really indifference to difference and is an effective way of smothering disagreement, and it denies its opponents even the satisfaction of martyrdom: it has been used by the Hindus to preserve their way of life intact in the fact of grim opposition."[202] He concludes the analysis of Hindu tolerance with these words: "Hinduism has no overriding moral attitudes but only spiritual aspirations."[203]

Other Indians have also challenged the myth of Hindu tolerance. Sarasvati Chennakesavan, for example, writes that "it is often claimed that Hinduism is a tolerant religion."[204] She continues, "Unfortunately, it is a historical fact that Hindus of the past did not show to the people of other faiths any real tolerance when vitally challenged. There were long years of conflict between Hinduism and Buddhism, between Vaishnavism and Śaivism, between Hinduism and Christianity. Within Hinduism itself, the imbalances between the castes as practised for several centuries, the suppression of the lower castes by the so-called higher castes, do not speak much for the tolerance of the Hindus."[205]

Bishop John A. T. Robinson in his book *Truth is Two-Eyed*, while condemning Christianity for failing to accommodate Hindu insights into its way of thinking and worshiping, adds that the oft-proclaimed "hospitality of Hinduism to all (or most) religious insights" is manifested only "on its own terms." This means that Hinduism tolerates other "religious insights" by "plucking them from their roots in the historical particular."[206] Thus, Hinduism is as "one-eyed" as Christianity.

"Spiritual fellowship is the meaning of history,"[207] declared Radhakrishnan in one of his prophetic moods. "Today humanity will be greatly enriched if the followers of different religions achieve justness in dealing with points of view which are not theirs and learn from each other."[208] But in one of his more temperate and less prophetic moods he praised Hinduism for its resistance to change: "Any attempt at a rapid passage from one set of rules to another would involve a violent breach with the past, and consequently confusion and chaos."[209] Anyone who has seen men standing in the Maidan in downtown Calcutta saying the Gāyatrī to the morning sun ("We meditate on that desirable light of the divine Savitri."), a prayer from Ṛg Veda 3. 62. 10, surmises that Radhakrishnan's warning against rapid change may be foolish. Even in philosophical discussions with Indian philosophers the Western philosopher is often stalemated by intolerance and unwillingness to work out differences. My own experiences have often confirmed the view expressed by N. Subrahmanian: "It was once aptly pointed out that in India 'a dialogue' usually means 'two monologues,' thereby suggesting the inherent inability of alien modes of thought or behaviour."[210] A persistent propensity of Indian philosophers—even today—is to quote an *Upaniṣad*, usually in Sanskrit, as irrefutable proof of the truthfulness of one's own pronouncements. Authority (*āgama pramāṇa*)—especially when shouted!—is superior to inference (*anumāna*) or observation (*pratyakṣa*). As for ap-

peal to the scriptural proof, Subrahamanian acknowl-
edges, "The Hindu scriptures have enough repertoire to
provide wise saws suitable for all purposes."[211]

Accommodation as a way to oneness of East and
West, despite the support of Radhakrishnan, does not appear to be a very likely technique. In the first place, accommodation may mean no more than the willingness to
let the other survive; and in the second place, accommodation talk may be only a way of earning foreign prestige.
These two negative evaluations apply to accommodation
whether the talk proceeds from the West or from the East.
The oneness that is needed in philosophy—as well as in
commerce, transportation, economics, politics, religion,
and elsewhere—transcends the minimal unity of a willingness to acknowledge the other's presence.

5. The Ways of Integration.

Fowler's dictionary calls the word *integration* a
"vogue word": To integrate is to combine components into
a single congruous whole. Psychology borrowed it from
mathematics and invented the expression *integrated personality*, a reasonable enough piece of jargon to describe
someone in whom, as Antony said of Brutus, the elements are rightly mixed by nature. The public have now
borrowed the verb from the psychologists with such
freedom that it has become a vogue word, habitually
preferred to less stylish but often more suitable words
such as *join, combine, unite, amalgamate, merge, fuse,
consolidate. Integral*, outside mathematics, is seldom to
be found except as the inseparable companion of *part*."[212]
An integration is an external relationship of parts. Oil and
vinegar when shaken in a cruet before being poured over
a salad are externally related. They form an unstable mixture. Salad dressing is an integration. Hydrogen and oxygen when brought together under certain conditions
form a compound known as water. A compound is far

more than an external relationship of parts. Water has characteristics not possessed by oxygen and/or hydrogen. Water is a synthesis. The return of water to its elements is not easy. The return of salad dressing to oil and vinegar is very easy. A new whole—a novel oneness—has come into being when oxygen and hydrogen combine to form water.

Failure to distinguish the terms *integration* and *synthesis* results in confusing statements. For example, "Significant syntheses will emerge only from persistent efforts to transcend limited points of view and to integrate partial truths into richer and deeper insights,"[213] errs in stating that syntheses emerge from integrations. Another example comes from an item in *The Times Literary Supplement* (London), May 3, 1944: "The metaphysics of Radhakrishnan's Absolute Idealism represents a real fusion of East and West." He is "the initiator of a new synthesis." But *fusion* designates an integration, not a synthesis. Moreover, Radhakrishnan objected to a fusion of East and West.[214] So did René Guénon. The last chapter of his *East and West* is titled "Not Fusion but Mutual Understanding." A fusion, he says, is "utterly impractical."[215]

Radhakrishnan has often been described as a "bridge" between East and West. Schilpp in the preface to *The Philosophy of Sarvepalli Radhakrishnan* conjectures it impossible "to find a more excellent example of a living 'bridge' between East and West than Professor Radhakrishnan."[216] D. M. Datta says Radhakrishnan's *Indian Philosophy* "acted as a veritable bridge between India and the West as well as between India and other Eastern countries where English is understood."[217] Joad describes Radhakrishnan as "bridge builder."[218] He also says that Radhakrishnan's conception of God is "a bridge between the religious thought of the East and the religious experience of the West."[219] Wadia refers to Radhakrishnan as mortar or glue; he is "a cementing link between the apparently widely differing cultures of the East and the West."[220] Charles Hartshorne also characterizes Radhakrishnan as an integrator of East and West—albeit less pictorially: "The thought of Radhakrishnan illustrates that convergence of traditions which some of us think to be one of the most hopeful signs in our world."[221] Saher regards Radhakrishnan and Aldous Huxley as "the ideal exponents of East-West integration."[222]

E-W symbolizes the way of accommodation. In accommodation Eastern and Western philosophers recognize each other, provide room for each other's influence, conduct dialogue, have fellowship with each other, discuss similarities and differences, and cooperate as far as they can within the limits of being faithful to their own traditions. In the oneness of accommodation no East-West philosophical mixture is fashioned. Integration is a way to a closer oneness. I symbolize integration as WE. The right line of the W and the vertical line of the E are identical, and the bottom line of the E is an extension of one of the middle lines of the W. In integration East and West find identical elements as bridges to each other. One significant metaphysical bridge could be the notion of the Absolute which appears in Taoism as the *Tao*, in Buddhism as *Śūnyatā*, in Neo-Confucianism as *T'ai Chi*, in Hinduism as *Nirguṇa Brahman*, and in the West as Parmenides' Being, Plato's Form of the Good, Plotinus's The One, Eckhart's *Gottheit*, Spinoza's *Natura Naturans*, Bradley's Absolute, and Tillich's Ground of Being.

In an integration of East and West the East remains East, and the West remains West. Each retains its status as a part of the whole. But in a synthesis of East and West the East ceases to be East, and the West ceases to be West. A new unit has replaced East and West. A full synthesis of East and West would remove from the self-knowing animal the existential anxiety which Teilhard designated as "a formidable crisis of individualism in the world, in other words, a counter attack by the shrinking, suffering, guilty, Multitude."[223]

Not all forms of integration are desirable. For example, the oft-heard remark, "There is only one God. We worship the same God in different ways" ignores the cultural determinations of deity. William Ernest Hocking humorously reports an "Indian reconciler of faiths" who brought together for adoration images of Śiva and the Buddha, a crucifix, a portrait scroll of Confucius, and a bust of W. E. Gladstone![224] In the worship hall of the Bahai Temple in Willamette (Illinois) and the great hall of the library of the Theosophical Society at Adyar on the south edge of Madras (India) medallions of the integrated religions are displayed high on the walls. One difference is that at Adyar the Masonic Lodge symbol is included!

Even in philosophical gatherings symbols can become confused. At the World Congress of Philosophy in Montreal (Canada) in 1983 an African philosopher was grossly misunderstood because many in the room did not realize that when he used the term *value* he meant it only in the Marxian sense.

The notion that a philosophy or religion can be—or should be—transplanted is one which many students of Eastern thought condemn. For example, Louis Renou writes, "When Hinduism is 'exported,' it tends to be regarded as a kind of theosophy . . . or a brand of Christian Science, tinged with pseudo-Vedāntism. It can only become a force for good in the world when it emerges in India itself as a purified religion free from primitivism and the cult of images. Extreme practices, such as *Haṭhayoga* and Tantrism 'of the left,' which often make a deep impression on Europeans, never constitute the main strength of a religion; they are special features that should not be imitated outside the land of their origin."[225]

Radhakrishnan often refers to integration as "cross-fertilization." Sometimes it is in the past: "There has been far more cross-fertilization of ideas than we are inclined to acknowledge."[226] Other times it is in the future: ". . . in the world of philosophy we have to bring about a cross-fertilization of ideas."[227] Often he indicates that it can come about through religions: "The different religious traditions clothe the one Reality in various images and their visions could embrace and fertilise each other so as to give mankind a many-sided perfection."[228] And at other

times—in this case in the same article!—he is less optimistic, claiming that the historical religions must transform themselves into a "universal faith,"[229] an "eternal
religion."[230]

Radhakrishnan's belief that the spiritual elements in
all religions will integrate the peoples of the world does
not take into account the disintegrating aspects of
modern life. How would he have responded to Barbara
Ward's analysis of the current religious situation? "When
. . . people talk about the confrontation of East and West
and the enrichment of our [Western] religious life by Eastern experience, they sometimes forget . . . that the East
has yet to face the disintegrating energies of Western
scientific and materialistic thought and that when the full
impact is felt, as it is beginning to be felt in China, it may
well be that less will be left of religious attitude in the East
than is left in Europe now."[231]

When Radhakrishnan says that the "components" for
the "new world" are all here, and that "what is lacking is
the integration, the completeness which is organic consciousness, the binding together of the different elements,
making them breathe and come to life,"[232] I feel an urge to
demand that he cut short the oratory and give some concrete suggestions. What does he mean by the term *integration*? How can the integrated condition be realized?
What should the West do? What should the East do? What
can I do? Nothing can be done until one knows exactly
what it is that should be done. Radhakrishnan might have
made greater contributions to oneness of East and West
through integration had he developed one methodology
of integration. For example, he might have traced more
parallelisms in Hindu and Christian cultures such as the
parallel of the *Hiranya-garba* (Golden Germ) in Ṛg *Veda*
10. 121. 1 and also the World Soul in *Kaṭha Upaniṣad* 3. 10.
11 and 6. 7. 8 to that of the Logos in the Fourth Gospel as he
did in *The Principal Upaniṣads*.[233] Parallelism is an excellent beginning to an anaylsis of integration. Hagime Nakamura has pointed the way in his book, *A Comparative
Study of the History of Ideas*: "This book represents an at-

tempt to isolate, describe and analyze certain key
philosophical problems that have appeared historically
in almost parallel developments within different cultural
areas, East and West."[234] The author adds, "By 'parallel
developments' I refer to the facts that in different areas of
the world similar problems, even if not similar concepts,
emerged at certain stages of cultural development."[235]
Nakamura closes his book with the hope that his investi-
gations "on the world history of philosophy will help contribute to a perspective of philosophical ideas with global
scope and bring about mutual understanding among the
peoples of the world, thereby fostering a concept of mankind as one."[236]

Nakamura's contribution to the integration of East
and West is more significant than to scold by telling us, as
Radhakrishnan does, "The different religions ... must
develop a spirit of comprehension which will break
down prejudice and misunderstanding and bind them together as varied expressions of a single truth."[237]

The notion that a religion, or the Hindu religion, or the
"spiritual" in religions can bind East and West into a happy,
fruitful integration needs to be examined objectively.
Judaism, Christianity, and Islam have checkered careers
as integrators of Western culture. The disruptive forces of
empirical sciences, democratic politics, naturalistic
philosophy, behavioristic psychology, and materialistic
value systems are now being felt in Eastern cultures. Do
Eastern peoples and Eastern religions have sources of in-
tegrative strength unknown among Westerners? George
P. Conger puts it very plainly: "But if, in any way, within
the limits proper to thinking, India can naturalize its
spiritualism and the West can spiritualize its naturalism,
there may be a profound and moving integration of
philosophies. ... With brilliant mind and glowing heart
he [Radhakrishnan] beckons us to seek it, even though
some of us must seek it in ways other than his own."[238]

6. The Ways of Synthesis.

Synthesis is a term with a positive connotation and ill-defined designations. It is a blessed word—whatever it means! Often it has a strange meaning. For example, a contemporary Christian theologian has written, "Christianity is not just one essential element in the cultural synthesis which Western civilization now so urgently needs. In principle at least, *it is that synthesis.*"[239] The reader discovers in the next sentence that *synthesis* in the mind of the author means "domination": "Only in and through the triumph of Christian thought can we hope to attain and enjoy a scientific social order which will use and glory in the achievements of science, and yet at the same time transcend the narrowness and pedantry of the merely specialized scientific and technical castes of mind."[240]

Charles A. Moore writes, "The spirit of Radhakrishnan's philosophy consists fundamentally in the attitude of synthesis."[241] If I were the editor of a journal on comparative philosophy, I would return a manuscript containing this sentence to the author with a note stating that *spirit* and *synthesis* are not allowed unless they are analyzed. If the author were Radhakrishnan, his answer would infuriate me, since the following is his definition: "If we are asked what the spirit in man is, it would be difficult to give a definite answer. We know it, but we cannot explain it. It is felt everywhere though seen nowhere. It is not the physical body or the vital organism, the mind or the will, but something which underlies them all and sustains them. It is the basis and background of our being, the universality that cannot be reduced to this or that formula."[242] Then he settled the issue with a quotation from the *Upaniṣads*: "That which one thinks not with the mind, that by which the mind is thought, know that indeed to be the supreme, not this which men follow after here."[243] A nondefinition and an unanalyzed quotation from an *Upaniṣad* is not satisfactory.

The word *synthesis* was the "vogue term" in the early issues of *Philosophy East and West*. Radhakrishnan often used *synthesis* in characterizing Hinduism, Indian philosophy, and the ultimate aim of comparative philosophical studies. The following quotations are representative:

> Hinduism is a large synthesis achieved in the course of the centuries.[244]
>
> Hinduism has synthesized all the foreign influences which invader after invader had brought to her from the outside, and moulded them to its own ideals.[245]
>
> ... the larger synthesis which alone can give the spiritual basis to a world brought together into intimate oneness by man's mechanical ingenuity.[246]
>
> [The world needs what Plato called] a synoptic vision [or what the Hindus call *samanvāya*, that is,] a philosophy which will bring the peoples of the world together and eliminate the conflict of the religions.[247]
>
> I do believe that the great idealistic tradition has in it the possibility of bringing East and West together in a closer union on the plane of mind and spirit.[248]
>
> [In an article published in *Modern Churchman* (October, 1922), he noted that Christianity in India] is attempting to combine the best elements of Hinduism with the good points of Christianity.[249]

In the General Introduction to *A Source Book of Indian Philosophy* Radhakrishnan calls attention to "the over-all synthetic tradition which is essential to the spirit and method of Indian philosophy."[250] He continues, "Indian philosophy is clearly characterized by the synthetic approach to the various aspects of experience and reality. Religion and philosophy, knowledge and conduct, intuition and reason, man and nature, God and man, noumenon and phenomen, are all brought into harmony by the synthesizing tendency of the Indian mind. The Hindu is prone to believe even that all the six systems, as well as their varieties of subsystems, are in harmony with one another, in fact, that they complement one another in the total vision, which is one. As contrasted with Western philosophy, with its analytic approach to reality and experience, Indian philosophy is fundamentally synthetic."[251]

Sometimes he tempers his arguments for a synthesis of East and West by saying he is willing to start with a lesser condition which he calls "an understanding." For example, "My faith is that human nature is everywhere the same and it has developed in different ways determined by the factors of geography and history. Now that the world has been drawn together by the forces of science and economics, there is need for understanding. I am not arguing for an eclectic synthesis but for an understanding which will gradually furnish the spiritual basis for world unity. I am persuaded that the new civilization, which is neither Eastern nor Western but world-wide, will build human relationships by means of the great instruments of science and technology on the basic insights of the spiritual value and dignity of man."[252] The need of philosophy today, he says elsewhere, is for "a world perspective which will include the philosophical insights of all the world's great traditions. The goal is not a single philosophy which would annihilate differences of perspective, but there must be agreement on basic perspectives and ultimate value."[253]

In his "Fragments of a Confession" Radhakrishnan decides to settle for "a world outlook": ". . . the stage is set, if not for the development of a world philosophy, at least for that of *a world outlook*."[254] He picks up the notion later in the article: "The new world society requires *a new world outlook* based on respect for and understanding of other cultural traditions."[255] This, he adds, remembering his education from ages eight to twenty in Christian schools, "involves an abandonment of missionary enterprises such as they are now."[256]

When is this synthesis accomplished? Is it a memory? A present experience? A future expectation? In his "Fragments of A Confession" it is a "perpetual wisdom,"[257] a "universal religion,"[258] a "*sanātana dharma*,"[259] a "fundamenal wisdom,"[260] "the eternal religion behind all

religions,"[261] a "timeless tradition,"[262] "wisdom un-
created, the same now that it ever was, and same to be
forevermore."[263] The synthesis appears in this context
to be a timeless reality rather than a temporal human
achievement. Yet somehow the human awareness of
this synthesis, which gives order and value to human
experience, has been lost. We must reach back to re-
trieve the lost original nucleus of religion and morality;
"It is our duty to get back to this central core of religion,
this fundamental wisdom which has been obscured and
distorted in the course of history by dogmatic and sectarian developments."[264]

In *Eastern Religions and Western Thought* he writes,
"We must recognize humbly the partial and defective
character of our isolated traditions and seek their source
in the generic tradition from which they all have
sprung."[265] Elsewhere he warns, "Our historical religions
will have to transform themselves into the universal faith
or they will fade away."[266] If one reads *The Hindu View of
Life* and *The Heart of Hindusthan* after reading this warning one concludes that Hinduism is the universal faith
and that all non-Hindu religions must be patterned after
Hinduism. This from the man who argues that the missionary enterprise should be abandoned! Sometimes it is
therapeutic to turn from Radhakrishnan's glorification of
Hinduism to an evaluation like M. N. Roy's: "What is
preached by Radhakrishnan as the orthodox Hindu
philosophy represents the intellectual reaction which
followed the fall of Buddhism and was galvanised by a
social stagnation lasting for the centuries of the Indian
Middle Ages."[267] I add to Roy's assessment my own conviction that Radhakrishnan's Hinduism shifts between a
Hindu scholasticism that appeals to śruti and a Hindu
gnosticism that appeals to a lost wisdom recoverable in
individual mystical experiences. This "eternal religion
behind all religions" that is preserved most purely in Hinduism is the heart and core of Radhakrishnan's philosophy. He may not have formed a system of philosophy
but he definitely had a theme to which he returned again

and again. Note the closing lines of his "Fragments of a Confession": 'The eternal religion, outlined in these pages, is not irrational or unscientific, is not escapist or a-social. Its acceptance will solve many of our desperate problems and will bring peace to men of good will."[268] He adds, "This is the personal philosophy which by different paths I have attained, a philosophy which has served me in the severest tests, in sickness and in health, in triumph and defeat. It may not be given to us to see that the faith prevails; but it is given to us to strive that it should."[269]

Those of us who sometimes have problems with Radhakrishnan-the-philosopher must constantly remind ourselves that philosophy for him is philosophy of life. Logic, epistemology, methodology, semiotics, ethics—even metaphysics—for him are propaedeutic to that philosophy-religion. He wrote in 1936, "The practical bearing of philosophy on life became my central interest from the time I took up the study of the subject."[270] I find difficulty relating his "eternal religion," which placed oneness in the past—a synthesis now forgotten by many, but preserved in the heart of Hinduism—with his notion that the unity of our hearts' desire is both a present achievement and a future expectation. For example, he closed his lectures at McGill University in October 1954 with this happy announcement: "We are living at the dawn of a new era of universal humanity. . . . The separation of East and West is over. The history of the new world, the one world, has begun. It promises to be large in extent, varied in colour, rich in quality."[271] He expressed the same optimism in his "Fragments of a Confession": 'The interpretation of obstinate cultural traditions is taking place before our eyes."[272] This seems strange, since on page 26 of this article he says pessimistically, "Today the world is very sick, for it is passing through a crisis of the birth of a new religion." In reading Radhakrishnan I often feel a desire to repeat James's advice to Royce: "You must study logic. You need it so badly!" Radhakrishnan, no doubt, would reply by reminding me that "consistent thinking is not creative thinking."[273] And I would reply by reminding

Radhakrishnan there is no evidence that consistency is prejudicial to creativity.

In another of the about-faces [274] for which he was noted he said in the opening address of the Second Seminar of the Union for the Study of the Great Religions in Madras in 1956 that "we are all interested in preserving the characteristic qualities of the different traditions and not letting them merge in a grey monotony."[275] In other words, synthesis is to be avoided, since in a synthetic religion each individual religion will lose its distinctive features. Yet elsewhere that is precisely what he wants to see happen!

Both critics and commentators have noticed and commented on Radhakrishnan's appeal to synthesis. For example, Joad says, "Synthesis and reconstruction are his objectives, and he believes that they can be most effectively achieved by a revival of religion."[276] Arapura says that "in Radhakrishnan we have a thinker who set himself rather deliberately and purposefully to the task of creating some kind of philosophical synthesis of the main streams of philosophy, Eastern and Western, particularly of the idealistic traditions."[277] Lawrence Hyde writes that Radhakrishnan "has contributed more powerfully than perhaps any other Asiatic to the immensely important undertaking of creating a synthesis between Eastern and Western thought."[278] He claims that for Radhakrishnan "the Hindu religion is an elaborate and flexible synthesis of a wide range of cults and beliefs."[279] Moore says Radhakrishnan is "the Thomas Aquinas of the modern age."[280] Moore praises his "ability and determination to see things in their comprehensive entirety and thus to eliminate the sharp distinctions which to the narrow and smaller mind serve as the basis for isolation and even contradiction of the several cultures and philosophical traditions."[281] Moore speaks of "his veritable genius for synthesis."[282] And S. K. Chatterji says, "Sarvepalli Radhakrishnan stands unrivalled today as the most convincing exponent of a Dynamic Hinduism which, true to its original character as a synthesis of diverse faiths and philosophies of life, is now offered as a Universal Doctrine capable of embracing the whole of humanity—as a *Sanātana Dharma* or 'Perennial Philosophy'—on which the wisdom and experience of the nations in the domain of the spiritual converge."[283]

John A. T. Robinson rightly notes that syncretism is not a value-free enterprise—and he correctly indicates that Radhakrishnan's syncretism is not without bias: "syncretism is as much a socially conditioned phenomenon as the exclusivism it opposes, often with a similar, if more subtle, spiritual superiority, such as often one cannot help sensing, for instance, in Vivekananda and Radhakrishnan in their judgments on Christianity."[284] Radhakrishnan's bias with respect to Christianity and to Western philosophies such as naturalism, rationalism, empiricism, and positivism takes the form "I'm more syncretic than you!" N. A. Nikam once described Hinduism as "the comprehension of a Truth which excludes nothing and no-body."[285]

The arrogance of Hindus, which many have noted, may be linked with the cyclical theory of time and the logic of nonexclusion. Linearity may be encompassed in cyclicism, but cyclicism cannot be encompassed in linearity. The logic of "either/or" may be encompassed within the logic of "either/or or both," but the converse is impossible.

Radhakrishnan's optimistic hopes for a synthesis of Eastern and Western philosophy and religion is not shared by some important thinkers both within and without India. I call attention to the opinions of Bhārati, Raman, Wach, and Malkani.

Agehānanda Bhārati, a European who has taken vows as a Hindu monk, thinks that a synthesis between Indian and Western philosophy can be only a compromise made by "popular philosophers," that is, "school philosophers" rather than "comparative philosophers." He writes, "It is said the time has come for a rapprochement between Indian and Western philosophy. In the form in which this statement has been advanced, it is probably nothing more than a trite pleasantry. We often talk of political and social rapprochements in order to bridge a gap in our conversations or business dealings, as an expletive, at parties or between nations. Personally I cannot but feel that, by such remarks, popular philosophies are doing not much more than uttering a truism. Two lines of thought cannot be reconciled without compromise on either side, if they are radically and technically different. If such a compromise is possible, it is a matter of indifference as to whether the two lines of thought have been hatched in one and the same place or continents apart. We have some misgivings about school-philosophers, therefore, who advocate this joining of issues. The stress is on *school*-philosophers, whom I distinguish from comparative philosophers. I would call him a 'school-philosopher' who has surrendered his mind to one particular tradition of philosophic thinking, and submit that all his further research must be biassed."[286]

N. S. S. Raman holds that synthesis of philosophies would be more difficult than the synthesis of religions— and they are far from having attained oneness: "The ambition to evolve a synthetic philosophy is, however, too unrealistic, and is comparable to the attempt to synthesize all the great religions of the world in a universal system of religious beliefs. In fact, the religions of the world may perhaps be more easily synthesized than the various philosophical systems."[287]

Wach maintains that "a 'world faith' on a syncretic basis is not a live option."[288] "Re-thinking" is fine. Synthesis of Hinduism and Christianity is impossible. He writes, "we are one with the Indian thinker in stressing the necessity of theological and philosophical 're-thinking' (to use W. E. Hocking's term) in the universal search for truth. But a combination in the sense of mere addition, even in the sense of a synthesis of the Hindu and Christian religions, seems unfeasible."[289]

G. R. Malkani says much the same—except he is speaking about philosophy rather than religion: "We conclude that a synthesis of Eastern philosophy at its best and Western philosophy at its best is not possible. But some interchange is certainly possible. The Indian can learn the method of presentation of the truth in a rational way, and the Westerner can learn the spirit of religious earnestness with which philosophic truth is to be pursued; and that is perhaps all that can be said by us on the subject."[290]

There are two fundamental flaws in the discussion of synthesis thus far: (1) no one has analyzed what is meant by *synthesis*, and (2) no one has indicated that there may be a variety of syntheses. At the beginning of the discussion of the ways of integration a distinction was made between integration and synthesis. Oil and vinegar may be integrated as salad dressing. Hydrogen and oxygen may be synthesized as water. A synthesis is a gestalt, that is, the whole is more than the sum of the parts. Salad dressing is liquid, and so are oil and vinegar. Water is liquid, but hydrogen and oxygen are not. Now a distinction must be made between two kinds of synthesis. A clue for the distinction is found in the observation of Eliot Deutsch that there is "a grand synthesis of world philosophy" and also there are "little syntheses."[291] A "grand synthesis," according to Deutsch, "usually turns out to be a matter of merely taking a series of ideas from one tradition and verbally harmonizing them with what is apparently contradictory to them in another tradition."[292] Deutsch does not describe "little syntheses," other than state they are formed to serve "a larger comparative end."[293]

D. M. Datta in an article titled "On Philosophical Synthesis" offers the following clarification: "Synthesis means creation of something new out of two different things, not necessarily opposites. As we shall see, not every reconciliation need amount to a synthesis, and not every synthesis need arise from conflict, and is not therefore, a reconciliation, though their spheres partly overlap."[294] Datta refers to "real syntheses." But he does not refer to unreal syntheses. A "real synthesis" has two characteristics: (1) it combines, and (2) it produces something new. Datta stresses the importance of novelty, but he muddies the analysis when he adds, "But there are also cases of real synthesis, attained, not by way of reconciliation or overcoming of . . . conflict . . . but by the spontaneous assimilation of various compatible ideas drawn from different theories, systems, and traditions."[295] Datta's Hinduism gets him into trouble in his elaboration when he confuses philosophical synthesis with mokṣa: "Real philosophical synthesis is marked by inner harmony arising from a steady and consistent vision and the resultant attitude with which ideas are selected, interpreted, assimilated, and transformed into a new theory of system. Real synthesis is reflected in the integrated personality of the thinker whose emotional and volitional life is only harmoniously organized, and is in tune with his emotional life."[296] Would Datta reject *Principia Mathematica* as a synthesis of logic and mathematics by reason of Russell's chaotic personal life? Datta's remarks, I should add, are consistent with Aurobindo's view that synthesis of East and West depends upon the West giving up its confidence in mind only and in accepting intuition as the way to "a consequent transformation of mind, life and body."[297]

Deutsch's "grand synthesis" and "little syntheses" and Datta's "real syntheses" and syntheses whose "spheres partly overlap" indicate that a distinction must be made between two types of synthesis.

In an East-West context one type of synthesis calls attention to certain elements from the East and from the West that are similar, compatible, or parallel and ignores those elements in each tradition that are dissimilar, incompatible, or contradictory. The aim in such a synthesis is to show that East and West do have common problems, assumptions, methods, conclusions, etc. Understanding, appreciation, tolerance of each other can be expected to result from this type of synthesis.

The other type of synthesis is more ambitious. The propounders or creators hope not only to preserve the values inherent in East and West but also to fashion ultimately a philosophy in which both East and West are transcended in a world philosophy. Those who support the possibility of this type of synthesis seek to form a new system of philosophy. This is what I call a gestalt philosophy, a philosophy which will surpass any current Eastern or Western system of philosophy. The example of hydrogen and oxygen becoming water might be improved by saying that a gestalt synthesis is what happens when a symphony orchestra translates black marks on paper into sounds in sequence that become experiences transcending that which can be spoken or written.

I have referred to the two syntheses in the list of twenty ways of oneness as synthesis *between* East and West and synthesis *of* East and West. The former is selective. The latter is inclusive. The former is one in which spheres partially overlap. The latter is one in which spheres coincide. The two may be indicated by the following two columns of near-synonymity:

Synthesis *between*	Synthesis *of*
incomplete	full
small	"large" (Radhakrishnan)
smaller	"larger" (Radhakrishnan)
"little" (Deutsch)	"grand" (Deutsch)
"eclectic" (Radhakrishnan)	total
relative	absolute
limited	unlimited
non-Gestalt	Gestalt
apparent	"real" (Datta)
partial	total

Raju is one who believes in the possible oneness of East and West which he calls "a world philosophy."[298] He writes, "If human life is essentially the same everywhere, if all values of life are to be made accessible to all men, then every culture will develop philosophies that bear essential similarities in thought, outlook, and aim. The aim of comparative philosophy is such a cultural synthesis, which implies not domination but development, not imposition but assimilation, not narrowing of outlook but its broadening, and not limitation of life but its expansion."[299] Raju leaves no room for doubt. He does indeed mean a total synthesis: "The comparative philosopher has to bring all traditions together and study all problems in their conspicuous forms. Then only will synthesis be fruitful."[300]

Moreover, Raju believes that this is the direction in which Radhakrishnan's work moves. He writes, that "if ever there is going to be a philosophical development out of both the Eastern and Western philosophies taken together ... Professor Radhakrishnan's work will be greatly used in the future and will mark a distinct stage in the history of the development of world philosophy."[301]

I, however, detect in Radhakrishnan's writings a less ambitious anticipation. For example, in his "Fragments of a Confession" he refers to the combining of part—the "best" part—of East and West: "The world which has found itself as a single body is feeling for its soul. May we not prepare for the truth of the world's yet unborn soul by a free interchange of ideas and the development of a philosophy which will combine the best of European humanism and Asiatic Religion, a philosophy profounder and more living than either, endowed with greater spiritual and ethical force, which will conquer the hearts of men and compel people to acknowledge its way?"[302] However, I may be underplaying the notion of the profounder philosophy that will lead to "the world's yet unborn soul." I confess that I have problems reading philosophy written poetically, and that I have serious doubts about a global philosophy.

I feel more comfortable with a philosophy made by selecting ideas from two traditions as M. N. Roy has done with Hinduism and Marxism.[303] Arapura has described some syntheses of Indian and Western philosophy as only a "selection of ideas": "Others proceed by making a selection of the ideas in Indian philosophy and orienting them towards an extrinsic end, an end that is brought in from outside its natural scope. The Marxists and the Thomists, among others, are busy doing this in their respective ways."[304]

S. K. Maitra, in his presentation of Sri Aurobindo's message, makes it appear as an argument for limited synthesis: "A synthesis between the existential or objective, and the axiological or spiritual standpoint,"[305] but it is in fact an argument for a full synthesis, as the following indicates: "This future philosophy will touch the whole of our being and not a part of it. It will not speak merely to our spirit or address our intellect or touch the sensuous part of our life, but it will have contact with the whole of our personality. Is it too much to hope that the East and West will join hands and work it out on the lines so clearly indicated by Sri Aurobindo? That is the consummation which Sri Aurobindo desired, and that is the true message of his philosophy."[306]

Robert Maynard Hutchins describes well a limited synthesis of East and West in his introduction to *Great Books of the Western World*: "We hope that editors who understand the tradition of the East will do for that part of the world what we have attempted to do for our own tradition in *Great Books of the Western World* and the *Syntopicon*. With that task accomplished for both the West and the East, it should be possible to put together the common elements in the two traditions and to present Great Books of the World. Few enterprises could do so much to advance the unity of mankind."[307]

We come now to the final step in the attempt to unpack the meaning of that confusing term *synthesis*. A synthesis *between* East and West is fashioned from selected aspects of East and West. A synthesis *of* East and West is fashioned from *all* of the East and *all* of the West. What the second statement designates is that some parts of either Eastern philosophy or Western philosophy are modified, changed, altered to make the synthesis possible. I do not mean "left out" or "omitted." That would be a synthesis *between* East and West rather than a synthesis *of* East and West. I shall use the word *distorted* to avoid any designation of omission. The word *distortion* has some negative connotations. For example, John N. Findlay commented one day at the Fourth East-West Philosophers' Conference, "I regard all wholly unifying philosophies as distorted and self-destroying."[308] But this is as it should be. One side must yield in the interest of total unity. My symbols are drawn to suggest that either the East is distorted to include the West, or the West is distorted to include the East, or both are distorted to include each other. The symbol indicating that both East and West are distorted is an ellipse. W. S. Gilbert called such "elliptical billiard balls," but the Greeks regarded the ellipse with its two centers as more beautiful than the circle with only one center.

Radhakrishnan's view of Hinduism may indeed by a synthesis *of* East and West in which the East is distorted to include the West. Wadia insightfully states that in his opinion the Hinduism which Radhakrishnan presents to the world is "something distinctive to himself; not quite the same as the Hinduism of history."[309] It is a Hinduism that has "a universal character; so that not merely a Hindu, but a Christian and a Muslim too can claim this Hinduism to be his own."[310] Wadia quotes from the Quaker periodical *Friend*: "If what he describes . . . really be Hinduism, then there are many thousands of Friends who belong to that religion, though they call themselves Christians."[311] I hypothesize that a similar statement might be made by a Western naturalist looking at Radhakrishnan's interpretation of idealism.

A synthesis of East and West in which both are distorted to include each is difficult to imagine. This seems to be what F. S. C. Northrop has in mind when he refers to "a new vision for our world . . . according to which both the Orient and the Occident enlarges its concept of the nature of things and of the spiritual, moral, and social man to include that of the other."[312] Perhaps this can be called "The Gingham Dog and Calico Cat Syndrome," since according to Northrop's "new vision" the East and the West just eat each other up!

Perhaps Moore is right! "The spirit of Radhakrish-nan's philosophy consists fundamentally in the attitude of synthesis." But we can now rephrase it: The psychological intention is to distort Hinduism so it becomes "a beautiful and invigorating humanism,"[313] a humanism shared by the West, a world where everyone has a nest.[314]

7. The Ways of Polarization.

The verb *polarize* and the noun *polarization* were first introduced in an article in the *Nouveau Bulletin des Science* on March 11, 1811. The author was Étienne Louis Malus, the French physicist, who had noticed that when looking through a plate of crystal at the sunlight reflected from a window the intensity of the light varied for differ-ent positions of the crystal. This led to his discovery of the polarization of light in 1809. The word *polarity* has since been adopted for wider denotations. *Webster's Third New International Dictionary* offers the following definition: "The relationship existing between two apparently op-posed objects that nevertheless involve each other usual-ly by being dependent upon a mutual factor (by day and night, or birth and death)." *Roget's Thesaurus* clarifies the word *polarity* by offering the following examples: "positive and negative; north and south; east and west; day and night; light and darkness; hot and cold; fire and water; black and white; good and evil; yin and yang; male and female." The difficulty I find in Roget's examples is that the conjunction does not imply that the two poles are "dependent upon a mutual factor." "Good and evil" are dependent upon values; "male and female" are dependent upon the reality of a living animal; "hot and cold" upon temperature. A hyphen might be better: "good-evil," "male-female," "hot-cold."

Polarity, according to Alan W. Watts, is "the two-sidedness of the one."[315] Eliot Deutsch unintentionally gives an excellent description of polarity when he describes Nirguṇa Brahman as "the name for the spiritual experience which harmonizes rather than obliterates distinctions."[316] Edwin A. Burtt, in a beautiful little book written when he was over ninety years of age, does not use the word *polarization*, but he describes an "exploring attitude" which "transforms what would otherwise be an irrational conflict of debators into a rational company of cooperative seekers for understanding."[317] Burtt adds, "Something like a generally accepted truth can take form out of the strenuous competition between many individual candidates for that position."[318]

I have attempted elsewhere to express my thinking on polarity. I begin with the analysis of duality.[319] According to my understanding there are two forms of dualism: polar dualism and nonpolar dualism. "In a nonpolar dualism the two fundamental realities are separate, independent, unique, and noncontiguous. The problem of establishing causal relations between nonpolar realities in a dualistic system leads to that peculiar form of agnosticism known as interactionism, or to that strange noncausal relationship known as parallelism, or to some equally unsatisfactory explanatory technique. But in polar dualism the two fundamental realities are both joined and disjoined. Polar entities are harmonious discords or contrasting concords. They are the extremities of a single whole. Whereas a void sunders nonpolar dual entities, the "space" between polar dual entities is filled. Poles are the necessary opposites of a single reality. Conflict *and* reconciliation are inherent in polarity. Nonpolar duals function as the existential application of the law of noncontradiction. Polar duals exhibit repulsion and attraction, rejection and acceptance, discord and harmony, strife and love.

"Nonpolar duality is illustrated in the Western pattern of good and evil. An unbridgeable gulf separates the two. They exclude each other. There can be no compromises. God and the Devil cannot establish a truce. Within

Christianity the importance of the Christ is that He and He alone in the awfulness of the Crucifixion met evil on its own terms and defeated it. Total warfare—a struggle involving complete elimination of one or the other—is the only possible relationship between good and evil. Redemption involves destruction of evil.

"Polar duality is vastly different. The negative and positive terminals of an electric cell or the magnetic poles of the earth are excellent examples. Without a negative pole and a positive pole there is no electricity. They oppose each other. They accept each other. And because of this harmonious opposition each is—and electricity is. There is always disquiet in the notion of a simple monism. Perhaps this explains the emotionalism of Parmenides, which required that he express his philosophy in a poem. Nonbeing cannot be—it is an absurd idea; yet Parmenides must have known he could not do without it. Nonbeing cannot be—but being cannot be either, save in the presence of nonbeing. The followers of Heraclitus always get the better of the followers of Parmenides, and the more Zenoes who arise to defend the master, the worse the situation becomes. Being can be only in the context of nonbeing, and nonbeing can be only in the context of being. One without the other is like a 'line' with only a terminus. No wonder the ancient Greeks preferred circles and ellipses to straight lines. No wonder Christians have had difficulty with the notion of one-directional immortality, that is, of a soul with a beginning but without an ending. As a Hindu friend once said to me, 'At least the Hindu conception of the soul with no birth and no death is less absurd than the Christian conception of an origin but no end.'"

Heraclitus, the first to introduce polarities in Western philosophy, by propounding such propositions as "The path up and the path down is one and the same," "God is day night, winter summer, war peace, satiety hunger," and "Things taken together are whole and not whole, something which is being brought together and brought apart, which is in tune and out of tune; out of all things there is a unity, and out of a unity all things,"[320] was awarded the nickname "The Obscure One."

The classical example of polarity in Eastern philosophy is the conception of the *Tao*. The *Tao* is composed of *yin* (the passive, the receiving, the negative) and *yang* (the active, the giving, the positive). But what is the nature of the composition? How are *yin* and *yang* related in the *Tao*? Are they parts of a whole? Symbolic expressions such as *yin* and *yang*, *yin* ⇌ *yang*, *yin*-*yang*, [(*yin* = *yang*) & (*yin* ⇌ *yang*)] are only approximations. Something like *yi/ang* is needed to indicate that *yin* and *yang* are both distinct from each other and also share in their natures. The familiar Taoist symbol of the two intertwining fish is ideal, indicating as it does by the black eye of the red fish and the red eye of the black fish that there is a bit of *yin* in *yang* and a bit of *yang* in *yin*, and that the two form a circle, the most perfect of all plane figures.

The logic of Hegel is an example of polarity. According to Hegel every thesis (statement) involves an antithesis (statement that appears to be contradictory to the original statement), which interacts polarily with the thesis such that a synthesis (statement which resolves the contradiction between thesis and antithesis) results.

Radhakrishnan interprets caste as an instance of polarity: "It [caste] is an illustration of Hegel's harmony of opposites, a point of view which reconciles the apparently conflicting claims of the individual and of society. Not the good of the self as a thing apart, or the good of society by itself, but a higher good, to promote which constant self-renewal and social service are the means is the governing principle of the caste system."[321]

His statement in *An Idealist View of Life* that the universe is one in which "evil, ugliness and error"[322] are "transmuted into their opposites through a gradual process"[323] may be another instance of polarization—and, I hasten to add, of optimism of a Pippa Passes order!

The most striking and clearest instances of polaric

thinking in Radhakrishnan's writings are in his early
book *The Philosophy of Rabindranath Tagore* where the
reader can never be sure whether the ideas expressed are
Tagore's or Radhakrishnan's efforts to read his own thinking into Tagore. Here are a few samples:

> The world of intellect, with its distinctions of good
> and evil, truth and error, self and non-self, beauty
> and ugliness, is only a stage on the pathway to real-
> ity. The intellectual vision is full of hard-and-fast
> lines of distinction. It makes the opposites absolute,
> and the system becomes full of contradictions; but if
> we pierce behind it we shall find that the rigid dis-
> tinctions of intellect are fluid, and mingle in a won-
> drous whole.[324]

> A true philosophy tells us that the distinctions be-
> tween the actual and the ideal, nature and art, life
> and criticism, and observation and reflection are rel-
> ative. The two become opposed when we draw a
> hard-and-fast line of distinction between the surface
> view of things, which we call the natural, and the
> deeper one which penetrates the veil, which we call
> the philosophical."[325]

> Intellect revelling in distinctions and opposites can
> give us . . . an unearthly ballet of bloodless categor-
> ies which is no substitute for the concrete riches of
> life."[326]

> [The universe is] a play of hide and seek between . . .
> God and man.[327]

There is no doubt that when Tagore wrote the following he was thinking polarily: ". . . the world in its essence
is a reconciliation of pairs of opposing forces. These
forces, like the left and the right hands of the creator, are
acting in absolute harmony, yet acting from opposite
directions."[328]

Raju may exaggerate, but he does not speak incor-
rectly, when he says that in Radhakrishnan "the old and
the new, in other words, East and West, are made to meet
without conflict. Both are presented as complementary
to each other."[329]

Others have decided that Hinduism is basically

polaric. For example, Koilpillai J. Charles says, "By portraying gods as imperfect beings, and man as capable of reaching heights of divinity and supernatural power, Hinduism emphasizes the overriding Māyā that govern this universe, and also brings out in a picturesque way the organic link between the positive and the negative, between the good and the bad, and between right and wrong."[330] Richard Lannoy in his impressive study of Indian life writes, "One of the most pervasive Indian views is that the entire phenomenal world is a balance of opposing forces (binal opposition). This dual organization is as fundamental to the Indian outlook as cell and sex divisions are fundamental processes to the biologist. As we have seen, in the daily life of caste society the commonest manifestation of opposition is that of purity and impurity. In traditional Indian thought the basic complementaries are form and flux, or order and disorder. . . . Everything in the complex social structure of India reflects this dual organization."[331] Likewise B. G. Gohkale contends that "in the history of Indian thought there is always an interplay of two opposite trends running parallel to each other throughout the ages."[332]

Our concern, however, is not whether Radhakrishnan interprets Indian culture in terms of noncontradictory dualisms but whether he regards polarity as a way to resolve the separation of Eastern and Western philosophies. Is polarization a way to oneness? In one place in his writings he seems to agree that it is: "We cannot overlook the different emphases not only between East and West, but in the different systems of the East as well as in those of the West. These differences are complementary, not contradictory."[333] The essence of polarization is poles whose differences are complementary toward the formation of a whole.

William S. Haas believes that the East tends naturally to polarity, whereas the West does not. The West tends to discern "irreconcilable opposites" which maintain "hostile antagonisms" to each other. The East tends to see "polarities" which "neutralize each other."[334] Haas's analysis is similar to Northrop's claim that in the East the emphasis is on "concepts by intuition," and in the West the emphasis is on "concepts by postulation." Northrop defines them as follows: "A concept by intuition . . . is one the complete meaning of which is given by something immediately apprehensible. . . . A concept by postulation is one . . . designating some factor in man or nature which, in whole or in part, is not directly observed, the meaning of which may be proposed for it postulationally in some specific deductively formulated theory."[335] The Haas-Northrop agreement may be stated as follows: Whereas Western thinkers recognize the rule of noncontradiction, Eastern thinkers do not. In the West if X is true, then non-X is false. In the East if X is true, then non-X may also be true.

Polarity is a relationship of two entities, attributes, values, or actions best described as attractive repulsion, conflictive harmony, divisive unity, rejective acceptance. Polarity is a dynamic condition of two in which negative processes, such as annihilation and domination, are balanced with positive processes, such as assimilation, accommodation, integration, and synthesis. In other words, in polarity the six ways of oneness thus far described are components. *Polarization* designates a process—not a substance, a movement—not a state, change—not fixity. Poles are both dependent on and independent of each other. Cold excludes heat, yet *cold* would have no meaning unless there were heat. Positive rejects negative, yet there is no positive unless there is negative.

A familiar polar relationship, which has not yet been mentioned, may be helpful in illustrating the facets of polarity. I refer to marriage. According to Christian Holy Writ a man and a woman become one in marriage. They enter the husband-wife polar relationship, a relationship in which one necessitates the other. The man-qua-husband requires the woman-qua-wife. The woman-qua-wife requires the man-qua-husband. A wife whose husband dies ceases to be a wife. She is a widow. The husband whose wife dies is a widower, not the "husband of a dead wife." *Husband* and *wife* thus denote a man and a woman in a relationship of polarity. Husband and wife are not self-existent realities. *Husband* and *wife* are polaric terms. The husband-wife relationship has been humorously—and accurately according to this polaric analysis—described as a cross between a dogfight and "the peace which passeth all understanding."

One of the common errors in thinking about the polar relationship is to consider the poles as two extremities of a continuum, forgetting that poles are existentially mutually dependent. This error is incorporated in an ancient Vedic myth. The gods appease Vṛtra, the dragon of drought, by agreeing to a charm protecting Vṛtra from death during day or night, in all places wet or dry, and from all weapons made of wood or stone. But Indra, the god of atmosphere, slew Vṛtra by attacking him at twilight (neither day nor night) on the seashore (neither wet nor dry) with a thunderbolt (neither wood nor stone). The error in the myth is in thinking of day-night, wet-dry, wood-stone not as polarities but as ends of continua. But these pairs are polarities. There is no nonday and non-night and no nonwet and nondry. (The impossibility of a nonwood and nonstone is obviously linked with an ancient metaphysics.)

There appear to be four ways of oneness in the polarization process based on what I shall call The Principle of Diminution. By *diminish* I refer to the fact that polarization is a process in which at varying times one pole is primary, dominant, stronger, and the other pole is secondary, subordinate, weaker. Part of the enjoyment of sweet-and-sour in Chinese cooking is located in the fact that the two flavors are not evenly mixed. One mouthful may be predominately sweet. The next may be predominately sour.

The four theoretical ways of oneness via polarization are: (1) pole A may be diminished; (2) pole B may be diminished; (3) both may be diminished; (4) neither may be diminished. However, the fourth theoretical possibility can be eliminated, since the essence of polarity is diminution. Poles depend upon each other, and dependence is a form of diminution. There is a positive only in a relationship of dependence upon a negative. A "positive" not diminished by a negative is no positive. A "marriage" in which both are first is no marriage. Both husband and wife would drive the same family car together, both would answer the same telephone together, both walk on the street side of the sidewalk, both hold the same pen while signing the same check! There cannot be a polar relationship without diminution. So there are only three possible polarities.

If *East* and *West* denote cultural poles, then there is no East without West, no West without East. I insist not only that East and West are poles but also that this is a desirable condition. A world with no East and no West would be what Radhakrishnan described as "a gray monotony." Those in the halcyon days following World War II who argued for a synthesis of East-West in a world philosophy did not take sufficiently into account the human consequences of such a synthesis. Did they want a world in which all human beings appeal only to concepts by intuition, or one in which all appeal to concepts by postulation? Did they want a world in which all are idealists, or one in which all are materialists?

The synthesizers, I suspect, think in terms of old-fashioned nineteenth-century nationalism—a nation as one people, one culture, one language, one religion. They may even think of a world of *my* people, *my* culture, *my* language, *my* religion. The ultimate of this mode of thinking is the Quaker mother who warned her son, "All the world is queer, save me and thee—and sometimes I have doubts about thee."

Institutions such as the United Nations, UNESCO, the East-West Center in Honolulu, and the School of Oriental and African Studies in London are significant institutions that help East and West understand and appreciate each other. Eastern and Western men and women should not cease being Eastern and Western, but they should cease being ignorant of each other. There are many ways of being human. Being unaware of other ways of thinking, feeling, valuing, and acting is not one of the ways of being the self-knowing animal.

8. The Way of Omegalization.

This is the way of ultimate oneness, a oneness transcending East, or West, or East-West. The term *omegalization* was coined by Pierre Teilhard de Chardin (1881-1955) to denote the telos of creation and the eschatological condition of the world according to the Christian revelation as interpreted by Teilhard. The term is related to omega, the last letter of the Greek alphabet. Sometimes Teilhard spoke of omicron, the fifteenth letter of the Greek alphabet, as the principle of natural unity and of omega as the principle of supernatural unity,[336] but usually he did not separate the material and the spiritual. The cosmic and the "Christic" were for him two faces of the same reality. *Omegalization* or *omegization* were the terms he used in the contexts of both science and religion. When he considered evolution only in a theological context, he used the term *Christification* or *Divinization*. When he considered evolution only in a scientific context, he used *cephalization* or *cerebration*.[337] These terms meant for Teilhard the process of making bigger and better brains.[338] Critics have accused Teilhard of merging science and religion, fact and faith, to form what may be called a *quasi-knowledge*.

The marvel of the twentieth century, according to Teilhard, is that the highest product of the evolutionary process has discovered the meaning and significance of evolution. "In us the evolution of the World towards the spirit becomes conscious. ... From this there finally emerges in our twentieth century human consciousness, *for the first time* since the awakening of life on earth."[339] Self-consciousness in this sense was not possible prior to Darwin. The result is that evolution is now at a crossroad: quiescence or progress? The only way forward is the way of total convergence—a way which will culminate in what Teilhard called the Theosphere.

Teilhard in his dual role as Jesuit and palaeontologist sought a synthesis of Roman Catholic Christianity and the theory of evolution. By *evolution* he meant "integral evolution," that is, evolution from chemical elements to atoms, from atoms to matter, from matter to life, from life to consciousness, from consciousness to self-consciousness, from self-consciousness to Omega. He also used the terms *spirit* and *Reflection* as synonyms of *self-consciousness*. *Reflection*, for Teilhard, designates the ability of the human being to focus the mind upon the thinking process. He liked to say "*L'animal sait, l'homme sait qu'il sait.*" (An animal knows, but man knows that he knows.) He used *Reflexion* when he wished to designate the biological coiling in upon itself of the human species such that no subspecies comes into being. *Omega, Omega Point, Point Omega*, and many other variations denoted the point of ultimate convergence, the final unity of integral evolution. "The more I look at life," he wrote, "the less I see of any other possible biological issue except the active consciousness of its unity."[340]

Julian Huxley agreed partially with Teilhard: "We both had drawn similar conclusions as to the unique position of man in the cosmos, and both were attempting to deduce something as to the probable future trends of human evolution . . . [but] I was quite unable to follow him in his approach to what he believed was the ultimate goal of evolutions' march, his so-called Point Omega."[341]

Teilhard wished to develop an approach to the universe and to persons in which there would be no shifting of view from the scientific to the philosophical and the theological. He called for an "inter-fertilization" of Christianity and evolutionary theory, a union which would be an undistorted expansion of the guiding principles of Christianity. In 1925 he was ordered by his superiors to give up his teaching at the Collège de France because of his views on evolution and original sin. From 1923 to 1946 he was in virtual exile in China where he worked as a palaeontologist. In 1948 he went to Rome hoping to accept the professorship offered him by the Collège de France and to receive permission to publish his manuscript *The Phenomenon of Man*. But he was denied the teaching post and forbidden to publish the work for which he said he had been born.[342] Although the Vatican squelched his hopes, the French Academy of Science elected him to membership in 1950. He died five years later.

Teilhard's life has been described as "a passionate search for unity"[343] and his thought as "a continuous search for unity."[344] He said that the whole adventure of his life was "to reach heaven by bringing earth to perfection. To Christify matter."[345] Some ecclesiastics felt he went too far when he closed his essay titled "The Spiritual Power of Matter" with a prayer to Matter: "Matter, you in whom I find both seduction and strength . . . I surrender myself to your mighty layers. . . . Let your whole being lead me towards Godhead."[346] In one of his last essays, "The Heart of the Matter," he offers the following maxim:

> At the heart of Matter
> A world-heart,
> The Heart of God.

Teilhard's stature has grown since his death. Joseph Needham calls him "the greatest prophet of this age" and "a prophet not for the Western World alone but for all men everywhere."[347] Ursala King writes, "Teilhard is one of the great Christian mystics of today but he is far too little known or understood."[348]

Teilhard called attention to a feature of integral evolution which he named the Law of Complexity/Consciousness.[349] This is the divergence that is manifest in the current approximately 2500 species of snakes, 4500 species of mammals, 8000 species of birds, and 1,000,000 species of insects. Yet there is only one species of man. Nature converges in the human. Man is "a species which converges, instead of diverging like every other species on earth."[350]

Teilhard wrote teleologically of a "directed evolution." The goal of evolution, he said, is spirit—a view that coincides with that of Radhakrishnan. Such language may have pleased some of his fellow priests but it distressed his fellow scientists. His religio-scientific style makes understanding difficult. Bernard Delfgaauw warns, "If someone has neither the time nor peace and quiet to seek to understand Teilhard's terminology in the context of its own frame of reference, he is bound to end up by failing to understand Teilhard's writings."[351]

I submit that part of the problem in understanding Teilhard is rooted in failure to recognize that his writings reflect his own growth. For example, he wrote in 1934 that he was pressing "towards horizons that are ever more shrouded in mist," in 1947 that "the sun of Christic energy has been steadily climbing to the zenith in my sky (intellectual and mystical)," in 1950 that he was experiencing "the blaze of universal transcendence,"[352] and in 1955, "I now live permanently in the presence of God."[353]

The natural world, according to Teilhard, has a unique intention for the human being. At the human level nature ascends to personality. Only a human being can say "I." Teilhard revised Aristotle's "Man is a rational animal" to "Man is a reflective animal." In the human being nature reflects on herself, humanizes herself, personalizes herself, deifies herself. In the human being evolution becomes self-directing. If the evolutionary progressive process continues, it will be by reason of human effort and human direction. "Man discovers that he is nothing else than evolution become conscious of himself."[354] Radhakrishnan states the same view: "Man's evolution is bound up with his conscious effort."[355] Man is in charge of evolution beyond man. Evolution from now on will be psychosocial, writes Teilhard.[356] The view might be stated as follows: Evolution prior to the appearance of the human being was cosmic-biological, and evolution after the appearance of the human being must be cosmic-biological-cultural.

Integral evolution will cease if human beings become unreflective. Reflection is an essential element of *Reflexion*. Teilhard feared that there are signs of human unresponsiveness in our century. He noted, "The great enemy of the modern world, 'Public Enemy No. 1,' is *boredom*. . . . I repeat: despite all appearances, Mankind is bored. Perhaps this is the underlying cause of our troubles. We no longer know what to do with ourselves."[357] The antithesis of boredom is research: "the highest human function . . . the supreme gesture of faith in Being . . . the highest form of adoration" is research.[358] Shortly before his death he said, "Less and less do I see any difference now between research and adoration."[359] His cousin, Mlle. Teilhard-Chambon, said of him, "The slightest hint of a new line of research, and off he went, however inconvenient or inopportune the move might be."[360]

Teilhard felt very keenly about the importance of research. In a paper written in the last month of his life titled "Research, Work and Worship" he reports that the advice the Roman Catholic authorities had given throughout his life was "Go quietly ahead with your scientific work without getting involved in philosophy or theology."[361] He adds the following revelation of the schizophrenic conditions which he suffered throughout his life: "To tell a religious to take up science, without at the same time allowing him in so doing, to re-think his whole view of religion, is indeed . . . to give him an impossible assignment—and to condemn him in advance to producing results of no real value, in an interior life that is torn two ways."[362]

The Omega Point is the goal of cosmic history. It is the converging of the many into the One. It is the return of the Christ at the end of time. *East* and *West* will be words without meaning. All will become one through the omegalization process. Omega, however, is not merely a possibility millions of years in the future. According to Teilhard, Omega is also supremely present. It is a goal that attracts and pulls, that guides and pushes. Omega is also alpha. Christ is both beginning and end: "Omega, He towards whom all converges, is concurrently He from whom all radiates."[363] Omega is not merely "a remote and ideal focus destined to emerge at the end of time with the convergence of terrestrial consciousness," but also it is "already in existence and operative at the very core of the thinking mass."[364] At the lower stages of evolution Omega acts "in an impersonal form and under the veil of biology," but now, by reason of the hominization process it is possible for Omega "to radiate from the one Centre to all centres—personally."[365]

Teilhard often refers to his favorite prooftexts from the New Testament:

Vulgate: "ut sit Deus omnia omnibus"
"God will be all in all"   (I Corinthians 15:28)

Vulgate: "in quo omnia constant"
"In whom all things hold together"   (Colossians 1:17)

Vulgate: "ut omnes unum sint"
"That they may all be one."   (John 17:21)

He does not interpret these as implying universal absorptionism. He was not a pantheist, as he clearly indicates in the following: "Lastly, to put an end once and for all to the fears of 'pantheism,' as regards evolution, how can we fail to see that, in the case of a converging universe such as I have delineated, far from being born from the fusion and confusion of the elemental centres it assembles, the universal centre of unification (precisely to fulfill its motive, collective and stabilizing function) must be conceived as pre-existing and transcendent."[366] Also he did not deny the reality of the many in the One. Donald Gray in his study of Teilhard writes, "Teilhard looks forward to the time when God will be all in all. Not that God will have then become the all or that the all will have become God, for at the most intimate stage of union the differences remain and are in fact heightened. In the end, the many will have become one in the One without, however, ceasing to be the many."[367]

Omega has four significant meanings in the writings of Teilhard. The simplest is the view that a time will come when the distinctions of race, culture, language, religion, and nation are no more. This is a completely secular approach to the awareness of the unity of the human species.

Sometimes Omega is interpreted theologically as a belief in a personal deity shared by all human beings that breaks down the barriers of suspicion among all peoples, overcomes the fear of death, and supports hope for an eternal condition of happiness. Teilhard points out, "Ever since Aristotle there have been almost continual attempts to construct 'models' of God on the lines of an outside Prime Mover, acting *a retro*. ['Starting from the beginning'] Since the emergence of our consciousness of the 'sense of evolution' it has become physically impossible for us to conceive or worship anything but an organic Prime Mover, *ab ante*. ['Drawing us ahead'] In future only a God who is functionally and totally 'Omega' can satisfy us."[368]

A third meaning of Omega is indicated by his use of *Christ-Omega*. Here he refers to Jesus the Christ as a transcendent personal center of human unity as presented in the Christian revelation and as accepted in the Christian community. Omega so considered should be recognized as referring to the office known as "The Christ," not to a human known as "Jesus." Teilhard makes the distinction by use of "Universal Christ" and "Historic Christ," and also by "the Word-God" and "the Man-Jesus." This use of *Omega* may be the most limited, since it designates only a Christian view. Teilhard says this is the view of John, Paul, and the Greek Fathers presented in the context of evolution.

Teilhard sometimes refers in his works to two Omegas: the Omega of "experience" and the Omega of "faith."[369] He also refers to two "Christs": "Christ-the-Evolver" and "Christ-the-Redeemer."[370] The former "bears the whole weight of the world in progress"; the latter bears the weight of the sins of the world.[371] He speculates that the two Omegas—and the two Christs—will finally be "synthesized."[372] He writes in a fuller statement, "Regarded *materially* in their nature as 'universal centres,' the Omega Point of science and the revealed Christ coincide. . . . But considered *formally*, in their mode of action, can they be identified with one another? On the one hand, the specific function of Omega is to cause the conscious particles of the universe to converge upon itself, in order to ultra-synthesize them. On the other hand, the Christic function (in its traditional form) consists essentially in reinstating man, in restoring him, in rescuing him from the abyss."[373] If Christianity can pass from the notion of "humanization by redemption" to "humanization by evolution," according to Teilhard, this would be the "starting point" of "a new theology."[374] Teilhard regarded his ideas as *fides quaerens intellectum* (faith seeking understanding), but the authorities at Rome regarded them as bordering on heresy.

The fourth meaning of Omega is expressed in Teilhard's writings as "Church-Omega." This was an effort to think of "the mystical body of Christ" in an ecumenism that would "include dialogue with the world."[375] This was an effort to shift the concept of the Church from an emphasis on sacraments and hierarchial authority to its role in cosmic-biological-cultural evolution. His ecclesiology was that of a "phylum of love" rather than an organized system of rites and creeds.[376]

The similarity between Teilhard's and Aurobindo's conceptions of evolution has been noted by many.[377] Joseph Veliathil notes that "Teilhard in the West and Aurobindo in the East are the first to grasp the immensity of the change in thinking to which [the] discovery [of evolution] must give rise."[378] Teilhard read part of Aurobindo's *The Life Divine* and commented, "This is comparable to my own work, but for the Indian tradition."[379] Aurobindo described the far-off goal of evolution as "a higher harmony and universality based upon conscient oneness with all existences."[380] But there is one striking difference: whereas Teilhard thought of evolution linearly, Aurobindo thought of evolution cyclically. Aurobindo adapted the ancient Hindu notion of Brahmā Day and Brahmā Night to a cosmic period of evolution and a cosmic period of involution. From Aurobindo's point of view Teilhard presents only half of the cosmic cycle. According to Aurobindo a period of many-ing of the One and a period of One-ing the many follow each other in an eternal systole and diastole.

Did Radhakrishnan entertain notions of cosmic unity similar to those of Teilhard and Aurobindo? The answer must be in the affirmative. I offer the following as evidence:

> When the whole universe reaches its consummation, the liberated individuals lapse into the stillness of the Absolute.[381]

> When movement reaches its fulfillment, life is not a going concern. The historical process terminates and individuals cease to exist as historical beings.[382]

> The Absolute is in this world in the sense that the world is only an actualization of one possibility of the Absolute and yet there is much in the Absolute beyond this possibility which is in process of realization.[383]

> The new birth for which humanity awaits is not a post-mortem salvation but is spiritualized humanity.[384]

> Man may be another unsuccessful experiment which the Unknowable, not quite sure of its direction, is making.[385]

> In spite of signs of design, there is a general trend in evolution toward specific forms not yet realized.[386]

> [All human beings are] destined to gain life eternal.[387] [All are to become] united by a perfect interpenetration of mind by mind.[388] [All are to be] filled with reality.[389] [And this state is to come] at the end of the world.[390]

Man is yet to become what he is.[391]

> The uniqueness of man among all the products of
> nature lies in this, that in him nature seeks to exceed
> itself consciously, no longer by an automatic or un-
> conscious activity, but by a mental and spiritual
> effort.[392]

> [Man is unhappy as long as he does not succeed in
> efforts to reach] an organic wholeness of life.[393]

Radhakrishnan warned against the tendency to over-
emphasize the individual self: "There is a tendency,
especially in the West, to overestimate the place of the
human self. . . . It is not realized that the thought of the
self which wants to explain everything, the will of the self
which wants to subjugate everything, are themselves the
expression of a deeper whole, which includes the self and
its objects. If the self is not widened into the universal
spirit, the values themselves become merely subjective
and the self itself will collapse into nothing."[394]

When Radhakrishnan was installed in the Spaulding
Chair of Eastern Religion and Ethics at the University of
Oxford in 1936 he gave an inaugural lecture in which he
said, "With the infinite patience of one who has endless
time and limitless resources at her absolute command,
Nature, slowly, hesitatingly, often wastefully, goes on her
triumphant way. She takes up an idea, works out its form
till, at the moment of its perfect expression, it reveals
some fundamental flaw, and then breaks it up again to
begin anew a different pattern. Yet in some way the wisdom and the spirit of all past forms enter into those which
succeed them and inspire the gradual evolution of the
purpose of history."[395]

Radhakrishnan closed his address titled "The
Supreme Spiritual Ideal: The Hindu View" delivered
before the World Congress of Faiths at Queen's Hall in
London on July 6, 1936 with these lines: "When the incar-
nation of God is realized, not only in a few individuals but
in the whole of humanity, we will have the new creation,
the new race of men and women, mankind transformed,

redeemed, and reborn, and a world created anew. This is the destiny of the world, the supreme spiritual ideal. It alone can rouse our deepest creative energies, rescue us from cold reason, inspire us with constructive passion, and unite us mentally, morally, and spiritually in a world fellowship."[396]

Radhakrishnan and Teilhard agree that there is a goal of evolutionary history, that the world will be created anew, that human beings are central in the realization of that goal.

Radhakrishnan expressed his faith as follows: "The meaning of history is to make all men prophets, to establish a kingdom of free spirits. The infinitely rich and spiritually impregnated future, this drama of the gradual transformation of intellect into spirit, of the son of man into the son of God, is the goal of history."[397]

Teilhard expressed his faith in the following credo:

> I believe that the universe is an evolution.
> I believe that evolution proceeds through spirit.
> I believe that in man spirit is fully realized in person.
> I believe that the supremely personal is the universal Christ.[398]

Charles A. Moore closed the Second East-West Philosophers' Conference with the injunction that Eastern and Western philosophers ought to move beyond "orchestrated unity" to "a real synthesis."[399] But philosophy is differently conceived in East and West. The term *philosophy* is Western. The Greek *philosophía* means "the love of wisdom." In the West *philosophy* designates human reasoning, rational judgments, intellectual discriminations. In China the term *san-ts'ai* (heaven-earth-man) is perhaps the best single term for philosophy. This term, which denotes three powers, forces, or origins is a reminder that in China philosophy is humanism. The human being has a status equal to heaven and earth. Philosophy in China deals with the relation of man to the natural world, to the social world, and to the world of spirits. Philosophy in Japan is called *tetsugaku*, a term coined when Western philosophy was introduced after the Meiji Restoration (1868). But philosophical thinking in Japan dates back to the sixth century C.E. when Buddhism was introduced in the island. In India *anu-iksiki* (the look of existing facts) designates contemplativeness and comprehensiveness of attitude toward total reality. To force Chinese humanism, Japanese Buddhism, and Indian metaphysics into a synthesis determined by Western philosophical assumptions would constitute a serious loss of variegated approaches to human life and thought.

I regard polarization rather than synthesis the *ēkata mārga*, the ideal way to the oneness of East and West. Omegalization remains a dream of oneness far beyond the imagination of most time-bound, rational creatures. The admonition of Vedic seers is still valid:

> *saṁ gacchadhvaṁ saṁ vadadhvaṁ.*
> *saṁ vo manāṁsī jānatāṁ.*
> *samānī va ākūtih.*
> *samānam astu vo manaḥ*
> *yatha vaḥ susahāsat.*[400]

Radhakrishnan translates this: "Walk together; speak in concord; let your minds comprehend alike; let your efforts be united; let your hearts be in agreement; let your minds be united, that we may all be happy." I offer as a transcreation: "May your intentions, your thoughts, and your dreams be harmoniously distinct, that a oneness with difference may prevail among you."

Notes

1. *Eastern Religions and Western Thought*, p. 308.
2. *East Versus West. A Denial of Contrast*. London: George Allen and Unwin, 1939, p. 247.
3. "Fragments of a Confession" in *PRS*, p. 7.

4. *The Brahma Sutrā*. London: George Allen and Unwin, 1960,pp. 7-8. But why did he say "even Western thinkers"? Eastern thinkers have also been parochial.

5. *Religion in a Changing World*. London: George Allen and Unwin, 1967, p. 16.

6. Ibid., p. 17. One cannot avoid noting that the denial that *East* designates a certain culture is not very convincing when stated by a man who wore a turban on public occasions!

7. *Eastern Wisdom and Western Thought*, p. 261.

8. *East and West*. London: George Allen and Unwin, 1955, p. 13.

9. In *East and West* Radhakrishnan makes the following sweeping unverifiable statements about truth: "Truth is of universal order" (p. 25). "The truth which is the kernel of every religion is one and the same" (Ibid.). "The truth is one and imposes itself on all those who know it provided they do know it with certainty" (p. 41). " . . . truth is beyond all expression" (p. 25).

10. Radhakrishnan. *Comparative Studies in Philosophy Presented in Honour of His Sixtieth Birthday*, p. 2. The editors were W. R. Inge, L. P. Jacks, M. Hiriyanna, E. A. Burtt, and P. T. Raju.

11. PRT, p. vii.

12. *Counter Attack from the East*. London: George Allen and Unwin, 1933, p. 53.

13. *Advaita Vedānta: A Philosophical Reconstruction*. Honolulu: East-West Center Press, 1968. Preface.

14. Radhakrishnan. *Comparative Studies in Philosophy Presented in Honour of His Sixtieth Birthday*, p. 3.

15. Ibid., p. 4.

16. Ibid.

17. Ibid.

18. Ibid.

19. Ibid.

20. Ibid. Arthur Koestler has written, "Rome was saved in A.D. 408 by three thousand pounds of pepper imported from India as part of the ransom paid to Alaric the Goth; ever since, when Europe found itself in an impasse or in a questing mood, it has turned yearningly to the land of culinary and spiritual spices." (*The Lotus and the Robot*. New York: Macmillan, 1961, p. 11.)

21. Radhakrishnan. *Comparative Studies in Philosophy Presented in Honour of His Sixtieth Birthday*, p. 6.

22. Edited by Sarvepalli Radhakrishnan and Charles A. Moore. Princeton: Princeton University Press, 1957, p. xxi.

23. Ibid.

24. Ibid., p. xxix.

25. *Hindu Intellectual Tradition*. Columbia, Missouri: South Asia Books, 1977, p. v.

26. "Radhakrishnan and Comparative Philosophy" in *PSR*, p. 678.

27. *An Idealist View of Life*, p. 16.

28. Ibid., p. 129.

29. Ibid.

30. Ibid., p. 135.

31. *Radhakrishnan and Integral Experience*, p. 6, footnote 16.

32. London: Kegan Paul, 1929, p. 90. Italics are mine.

33. *Philosophy East and West*, Vol. 9, No. 3, 1960, pp. 107-128.

34. "On Philosophical Synthesis." *Philosophy East and West*, Vol. 13, No. 3, 1963, pp. 195-196.

35. *Philosophy East and West*, Vol. 1, No. 1, 1951, p. 3. Compare the following from Hajime Nakamura: "I wish to avoid the old dichotomy of East and West. The East is not a cultural unit; it consists of various cultural areas. For example, although we cannot deny some points of similarity, Japanese culture is radically different from Indian culture. When a clear and specific statement is needed, this dichotomy will not be used. On occasion, of course, the conventional appellation will be used for convenience of exposition; and on such occasions, by 'West' I mean the tradition of Graeco-Judaic-Christian thought, and by 'East' I mean chiefly the traditions of India, China, Japan, etc." (*A Comparative History of Ideas*. London: Kegan Paul, 1986, p. 4. First published in Tokyo in 1975.)

36. Ibid., p. 4.

37. Ibid., p. 5.

38. Ibid.

39. Ibid., pp. 6-9.

40. Ibid., p. 15.

41. *Philosophy East and West*, Vol. 1, No. 4, 1952, p. 5.

42. Ibid.

43. *Philosophy East and West*, Vol. 1, No. 4, 1952, p. 44.

44. *A Source Book in Indian Philosophy*, p. xxv.

45. "Dynamic Hinduism and Radhakrishnan" in *PSR*, p. 483. Others make the same claim for Christianity. For example, J. V. Langmead Casserley contends, "Christian thought in our civilization is the essential and indispensable organ of cultural synthesis." (*The Retreat from Christianity in the Modern World*. London: Longmans, Green, 1952, p. 163.)

46. S. K. Maitra, *The Meeting of East and West in Sri Aurobindo's Philosophy*. Pondicherry: Sri Aurobindo Ashram, 1956, p. 32.

47. *Eastern Religions and Western Thought*, p. 2.

48. *East and West*, p. 25.

49. *Eastern Religions and Western Thought*, p. viii.

50. Ibid., p. vii.

51. A. R. Wadia in Radhakrishnan. *Comparative Studies in Philosophy Presented in Honour of His Sixtieth Birthday*, p. 87.

52. G. P. Conger in Ibid., p. 313.

53. *Counter Attack from the East*, p. 34.

54. "Fragments of a Confession" in *PSR*, p. 25.

55. New York: Dell Publishing Co., 1968.

56. Springfield, Illinois: G. and C. Merriam Co., 1973. First published in 1942.

57. Ibid., p. 23a.

58. Ibid., p. 24a.

59. Ibid.

60. Ibid.

61. Ibid., p. 30a.

62. Ibid.

63. Ibid.

64. *International Review of Missions*, July 1913, p. 522.

65. London: The Centenary Press, 1939, p. 13.

66. Ibid.

67. Ibid.

68. *Science and Christ*. Tr. René Hague. London: Collins, 1965, p. 108.

69. Ibid., p. 111.

70. Ibid.

71. Ibid., p. 126.

72. *The Knowledge of God and the Service of God According to the Teaching of the Reformation*. Trs. J. L. M. Haire and Ian Henderson. London: Hodder and Stoughton, 1938, pp. 43-44.

73. See *International Review of Missions*. June 1942, p. 842.

74. Tr. Olive Wyon. London: Lutterworth Press, 1934, p. 33.

75. Ibid., p. 25.

76. See p. 25, footnote 1.

77. Ibid., p. 34.

78. Ibid., p. 38.

79. Ibid., p. 40.

80. Ibid.

81. *East and West*. Tr. William Massey. London: Luzac, 1941, p. 135.

82. Ibid. Western contact with the "mysterious East" has sometimes been humorous. I recall two examples from my years in India. One was my puzzlement when, upon purchasing a small kerosene pump at an Indian village market, I discovered the words "Gift of the People of the USA" stamped on

it. I learned that during a famine tins of Wisconsin cheese had been sent to West Bengal. The Indians, disliking the taste of the cheese, fed the cheese to goats and made ingenious items out of the tin. The other was told to me by a Bengali village worker. He said that a shopkeeper in the 1940s refused to sell him an item because, as he said, "I can get more from the damn cheap sahibs." My friend, upon discovering that the merchant was referring to American soldiers, shamed him for using such language to describe the soldiers. The merchant replied, "When come to my shop they always say 'Damn cheap! I'll buy it.'" Sometimes the converter-converted relationship has a financial dimension. A relative of mine, who had been a missionary in the Orient for many years, often used the expression "We came to do good, and we did well." He should know. He invested in a coconut plantation which, when the trees started producing, yielded annual income of 100% of the investment during the life of the trees.

83. *Harijan*, May 14, 1936.

84. Ronald W. Clark, *The Life of Bertrand Russell*. Harmondsworth: Penguin, 1975, p. 489.

85. *Eastern Religions and Western Thought*, p. 341, footnote 1.

86. "Radhakrishnan and Comparative Philosophy" in *PSR*, p. 672.

87. Ibid., p. 681. Lest Christians feel that Radhakrishnan was unfair in his condemnation of Christianity they might note that the brilliant Michael Servetius was put to death by John Calvin in Geneva on October 27, 1553 in accordance with the order of the papal authorities that the heretic was "to be taken, together with his books, on a timbril, or dust-cart, to the place of execution, and there burned alive *by a slow fire* until his body is reduced to ashes." (David Cuthbertson, *A Tragedy of the Reformation*. Edinburgh: Oliphant, Anderson, and Ferrier, 1912, p. 45.) Servitius was put to death on two counts: anti-Trinitarianism and anti-paedobaptism.

88. Ibid., p. 40.

89. *Occasional Speeches and Writings. February 1956-February 1957*. New Delhi: The Publications Division, Ministry of Information and Broadcasting, Government of India, 1957, p. 251.

90. *Religion and the Christian Faith*. London: Lutterworth Press, 1956, p. 121.

91. *The Christian Faith and Other Faiths*. London: Oxford University Press, 1961, p. 82.

92. *PRT*, p. 177.

93. *East and West*. International League of International Co-operation. League of Nations, 1935, p. 40.

94. Ibid., p. 63.

95. *Occasional Speeches and Writings. October 1952-February 1959*, p. 335.

96. *Eastern Religions and Western Thought*, p. 326.

97. "Radhakrishnan and the Comparative Study of Religion" in PSR, p. 451.

98. London: George Allen and Unwin, 1940, p. 143.

99. Ibid., p. 145. Quoted by Nicol Macnicol, *British Weekly*, March 30, 1933.

100. *Living Religions and a World Faith*, p. 172.

101. Ibid.

102. "My Search for Truth" in *Religion in Transition*, p. 11.

103. "Fragments of a Confession" in PSR, p. 6.

104. Ibid., p. 9.

105. Ibid., p. 73.

106. Ibid., p. 74. Although Radhakrishnan was opposed to all Christian missionary efforts, his friend A. R. Wadia refers to "the missionary zeal" with which Radhakrishnan "defends Hinduism" and to his "missionary zeal to carry the message of India to the West." ("The Social Philosophy of Radhakrishnan" in PSR, pp. 757, 759.)

107. "Fragments of a Confession" in PSR, p. 73.

108. Ibid., p. 74.

109. Ibid.

110. Ibid.

111. *Religions in Ancient India*. London: Athlone Press, 1953, p. 55. See also p. 109.

112. *The Vedanta Sutras with the Commentary of Ramanuja. Sacred Books of the East*, Vol. 48. Tr. George Thibaut. Oxford: Clarendon Press, 1904, pp. 33, 37.

113. Ibid., p. 34.

114. Ibid., p. 39.

115. *Eastern Religions and Western Thought*, p. 306.

116. Ibid.

117. Ibid.

118. Third edition. London: Oxford University Press, 1958, p. 107. The reference, of course, is to Machiavelli's treatise. Selections from the *Arthaśāstra* are included in *A Source Book in Indian Philosophy* (pp. 193-223), but the work has been so carefully bowdlerized that the reader is unaware of its Machiavellian nature.

119. *The Bhagavadgītā*. London: George Allen and Unwin, 1948, p. 68.

120. *PRT*, p. 200.

121. *Eastern Religions and Western Thought*, p. 308.

122. Ibid.

123. *The Hindu View of Life*, p. 34.

124. "Radhakrishnan's Influence on Indian Thought" in *PSR*, p. 525.

125. *The Speaking Tree*. London: Oxford University Press, 1971, p. 13.

126. *Introduction to the Study of Hindu Doctrines*. Tr. Marco Pallis. London: Luzac, 1945, p. 19. But Guénon does not want the West to assimilate! He writes that "there is only one way for the West to make itself bearable: that is . . . that it should give up 'assimilation' and practice instead 'association.' " (*East and West*, p. 45.)

127. London: SCM Press, 1979.

128. Ibid., p. 7.

129. *The Heart of Hindusthan*. Madras: Natesan, 1936, pp. 25-26.

130. Ibid., pp. 52-53.

131. Ibid., p. 49.

132. Ibid., p. 51.

133. *The Indian Concept of Values*. New Delhi: Manohar, 1978, p. 5.

134. *The Destiny of the Mind: East and West*. London: Faber and Faber, 1956, p. 285.

135. Ibid., pp. 285-286.

136. Ibid., pp. 42-43.

137. Ibid., p. 43.

138. *Religions of Ancient India*, pp. 106-107.

139. *Young India*, June 26, 1924.

140. "Swaraj in Ideas." *Visvabharati Quarterly*, Vol. 25, Nos. 3 and 4, 1960, p. 300.

141. *East and West*, p. 134.

142. Ibid., p. 226.

143. *The Destiny of the Mind: East and West*, p. 281.

144. *Hinduism*. London: Chatto and Windus, 1979, p. 8. Chaudhuri says that Aldous Huxley is "a pitiful example" of a Westerner who tried to find mental stability and spiritual confidence in Hinduism.

145. Tr. Roland Hindmarsh. London: Burns and Oates, 1960, p. 10. Published originally in French in 1956.

146. Ibid., pp. 17-18. This book carries both the *Nihil obstate* and the *Imprimatur*. The volumes *Christian Zen* by Willard Johnson (New York: Harper and Row, 1971) and *Christian Yoga and You* by E. Alexandrou (San Jose, California: Christananda Publishing Co., 1975) should also be consulted.

147. *Kalki; or, The Future of Civilization*. London: Kegan Paul, 1929, p. 92.

148. Eusebius, *Historia Ecclesiastica*, book 9, chap. 9. See Maude Aline Huttmann, *The Establishment of Christianity and the Proscription of Paganism*. New York: Columbia University Press, 1914, p. 18. Constantine was not noted for his humility. Robert Lopez writes, "Constantine would not have objected to being told that he had changed the course of history." (*Encyclopedia Britannica*, 15th edition. Vol. 5, p. 74.)

149. Eusebius, *Vitae Sophistarum*, book 4, chap. 8, note 2. See Huttmann, *The Establishment of Christianity and the Proscription of Paganism*, p. 64.

150. Huttmann, *The Establishment of Christianity and the Proscription of Paganism*, p. 139.

151. 16:6b. King James Version.

152. *Truth is Two-Eyed*, p. 131. Among the many books on India and Christianity I recommend the following: *India and the Latin Captivity of the Church* by Robin H. S. Boyd (London: Cambridge University Press, 1974); *An Introduction to Indian Christian Theology* by Robin H. S. Boyd (Madras: Christian Literature Society, 1969); *Christ and Hindu in Vrindaban* by Klaus Klostermaier (London: SCM Press, 1969).

153. *Truth is Two-Eyed*, p. 131.

154. Ibid., pp. 131-132.

155. Eusebius, *Life of Constantine* 3. 20. See Christopher Bush Coleman, *Constantine the Great and Christianity*. New York: Columbia University Press, 1914, p. 71.

156. See Huttman, *The Establishment of Christianity and the Proscription of Paganism*, pp. 127-149 for English translations of these laws.

157. Ibid., p. 240.

158. James Cochran Stevenson Runciman, *A History of the Crusades, Vol. 3*. Cambridge: Cambridge University Press, 1954, p. 480.

159. *The Retreat from Christianity in the Modern World*, pp. 54-55.

160. Ibid., p. 174.

161. *India and the Latin Captivity of the Church*, p. 4.

162. Mary Lukas and Ellen Lukas, *Teilhard*. London: Collins, 1977, p. 73.

163. "Letters to Léontine Zanta" in R. C. Zaehner, *Evolution in Religion*. Oxford: Clarendon Press, 1971, pp. 17-18. Italics are mine.

164. *Oeuvres*, ii.

165. *Occasional Speeches and Writings. October 1952-January 1956*. New Delhi: The Publication Division, Min-

istry of Information and Broadcasting, Government of India, 1956, p. 237.

166. *An Idealist View of Life*, p. 274.

167. *Eastern Religions and Western Thought*, p. 345.

168. *Is This Peace?*, p. 72.

169. Ibid. Urumpackal in *Organized Religion According to Dr. S. Radhakrishnan*, p. 221 observes that Radhakrishnan condemns Christian domination (for example, *Eastern Religions and Western Thought*, p. 10) and praises Hindu and Buddhist domination (for example, *The Hindu Way of Life*, p. 90).

170. P. 12. See also *Eastern Religions and Western Thought*, pp. 335f.

171. See "Reason and Intuition in Radhakrishnan's Philosophy" in *PSR*, p. 176.

172. *The Bleeding Heart*. Ed. Shri Ramnath Suman. Ajmer: Sasta-Sahitya Press, 1933, p. 5.

173. P. 280.

174. *Comparative Philosophy*. New York: Harcourt Brace, 1926, p. 44.

175. Ibid., p. 50.

176. P. T. Raju, *Idealistic Thought in India*. London: George Allen and Unwin, 1953, p. 332.

177. "Radhakrishnan and the Religion of Spirit" in *PSR*, p. 332.

178. *Idealistic Thought in India*, pp. 331-332.

179. *The Heart of Hindusthan*, pp. 51-52.

180. *Eastern Religions and Western Thought*, p. 313.

181. Ibid., p. 317.

182. Ibid., p. 57. Why do Indian philosophers lapse into poetic sentimentalisms? For example, N. S. S. Raman has written, "As India has tolerated many religions on its soil, it can also 'let many flowers bloom' in the field of philosophy." ("Is Comparative Philosophy Possible?" in *Indian Philosophy Today*. Ed. N. K. Devaraja. Delhi: Macmillan Co. of India, 1975, p. 201.)

183. Ibid., p. 335.

184. Ibid., p. 320.

185. *The Hindu View of Life*, p. 36.

186. Ibid., p. 25.

187. Ibid., p. 44.

188. Ibid., p. 16.

189. Ibid., p. 32.

190. Ibid., p. 37.

191. *A Shortened History of England*. Harmondsworth: Penguin Books, 1958, p. 353.

192. *Indian Philosophy*, Vol. 2, p. 775.

193. Ibid.
194. Ibid.
195. P. 322.
196. *The Hindu Tripod and Other Essays.* Madurai: Hookal Publishers, 1976, p. x.
197. Ibid., p. 15.
198. Ibid., pp. 15-16.
199. Ibid., p. 17.
200. Ibid., pp. 17-18.
201. Ibid., p. 18.
202. Ibid., p. 19.
203. Ibid.
204. *A Critical Study of Hinduism.* London: Asia Publishing House, 1974, p. x.
205. Ibid.
206. P. 103.
207. *A Seminar on Saints*, p. 2.
208. Ibid.
209. *The Heart of Hindusthan*, p. 4.
210. *The Hindu Tripod and Other Essays*, p. 117, footnote 13.
211. Ibid., p. 69, footnote 60.
212. H. M. Fowler, *A Dictionary of Modern English Usage.* Oxford: Clarendon Press, 1952, p. 289. The psychological designation of *integration* is important, but it is not relevant to the oneness considered in this study. Louis Renou closed a series of three lectures on Hinduism at the School of Oriental and African Studies (London) in May 1951 with the comment that in Hinduism there is "an underlying principle that given favourable conditions, may well lead to a new integration of human personality." (*Religions of Ancient India*, p. 110.) Radhakrishnan refers to "integral thinking," which he describes as "thinking with one's whole mind and one's whole body." (*East and West in Religion.* London: George Allen and Unwin, 1933, p. 81.)
213. Bernard Phillips, "Radhakrishnan's Critique of Naturalism" in *PSR*, p. 118. Phillips is correct when he writes, "Juxtaposition is not integration." (Ibid.) In my terminology this would be "Accommodation is not integration."
214. See "Fragments of a Confession" in *PSR*, pp. 75-77.
215. P. 219.
216. P. xi.
217. "Radhakrishnan and Comparative Philosophy" in *PSR*, p. 673.
218. *Counter Attack from the East*, pp. 38-39.
219. Ibid., p. 130.

220. "The Social Philosophy of Radhakrishnan" in *PSR*, p. 757.

221. "Radhakrishnan on Mind, Matter and God" in *PSR*, p. 322.

222. See *Eastern Wisdom and Western Thought*, pp. 41-44.

223. Pierre Teilhard de Chardin, *Writings in Time of War*. Tr. René Hague. London: Collins, 1968, p. 105.

224. *Living Religions and a World Faith*, p. 181. This may not be as absurd as it appears to be. The Jesuit palaeontologist, Pierre Teilhard de Chardin, kept a representation of the Sacred Heart of Jesus and a picture of Galileo side by side on his desk in the Institute of Geo-Biology in Peking. (See Lukas and Lukas, *Teilhard*, p. 175.)

225. *Religions of Ancient India*, p. 109.

226. *East and West*, p. 17.

227. "Fragments of a Confession" in *PSR*, p. 13.

228. Ibid., p. 76.

229. Ibid., p. 81.

230. Ibid., p. 82.

231. *The Interplay of East and West*. London: George Allen and Unwin, 1957, pp. 78-79. I was made aware of this in India when an Indian graduate student asked me why I was studying Hinduism, since "it is being kept alive in India by only sentimental old women."

232. *Eastern Religions and Western Thought*, p. 19.

233. London: George Allen and Unwin, 1953, pp. 61-62.

234. P. 3.

235. Ibid.

236. Ibid., p. 567.

237. *Eastern Religions and Western Thought*, p. 306.

238. "Radhakrishnan's World" in *PSR*, pp. 110-111.

239. J. V. Langmead Casserley, *The Retreat from Christianity*, p. 89. Italics are Casserley's.

240. Ibid. How the synthesis of scientific technology and social order hinges on the triumph of Christian thought over Hindu, Buddhist, Confucian, Taoist, humanistic, atheistic, Communistic, and all other forms of thought is not clear to me!

241. "Radhakrishnan's Metaphysics and Ethics" in *PSR*, p. 382.

242. *An Idealist View of Life*, p. 205.

243. Ibid. The quotation is *Kena Upaniṣad* 1. 5.

244. *Eastern Religions and Western Thought*, p. 339. Radhakrishnan says that Indian philosophy has seven "attributes":

> 1. "concentration upon the spiritual" (*A Source Book of Indian Philosophy*, p. xx.)
> 2. "belief in the intimate relationship of philosophy

and life" (Ibid.)

3. "introspective approach to reality" (Ibid., p. xxii.)

4. "tendency ... in the direction of monistic idealism" (Ibid., p. xxiii.)

5. "unquestioned and extensive use of reason, but intuition is accepted as the only method through which the ultimate can be known" (Ibid.)

6. "acceptance of authority" (Ibid., p. xxiv.) He says that in Indian philosophy "the Scholastic Period is still in progress." (Ibid., p. xix.)

7. "synthetic approach to the various aspects of experience and reality" (Ibid., p. xxv.)

245. *PRT*, p. 200.

246. *Eastern Religions and Western Thought*, p. 348.

247. *An Idealist View of Life*, p. 83.

248. "Reply to Critics" in *PSR*, p. 804.

249. The essay is reprinted in *The Heart of Hindusthan*, pp. 89-122. The quotation is on page 122. In the Jowett lecture given on March 18, 1930 at the Mary Ward Settlement in London Radhakrishnan reversed himself. He said, "Today when Christianity is faced by the religion of India, it is adopting an attitude of unbending self-sufficiency. It has lost the features of teachability and tolerance which characterized it in its early days." (*East and West in Religion*, p. 64.)

250. P. xxv.

251. Ibid. Notice that here, as elsewhere, Radhakrishnan seems to identify Indian philosophy and Hindu religion.

252. Foreword to P. Kodanda Rao, *East Versus West*, pp. 7-8.

253. *A Source Book in Indian Philosophy*, p. xxix.

254. *PSR*, p. 13. Italics are mine.

255. Ibid., p. 73. Italics are mine.

256. Ibid., p. 74.

257. Ibid., p. 80.

258. Ibid.

259. Ibid. *Sanātana dharma* is a very important term in Hinduism. *Sanataña* means "ancient" or "eternal." It connotes sacredness by reason of antiquity. *Dharma* has three meanings, depending upon the context:

1. The principle of order in the physical world.

2. The precepts of approved moral behavior.

3. The moral ideal by which human behavior is judged as good or bad and as right or wrong.

260. Ibid.

261. Ibid.

262. Ibid.

263. Ibid. A quotation from St. Augustine.

264. Ibid.

265. P. 347.

266. "Fragments of a Confession" in *PSR*, p. 81.

267. "Radhakrishnan in the Perspective of Indian Philosophy" in *PSR*, p. 564.

268. *PSR*, p. 82.

269. Ibid.

270. "The Spirit in Man" in *Contemporary Indian Philosophy*. Revised edition. Eds. S. Radhakrishnan and J. H. Muirhead. London: George Allen and Unwin, 1952, p. 475. First published in 1936.

271. *East and West*, pp. 130, 131.

272. *PSR*, p. 73.

273. "The Spirit in Man" in *Contemporary Indian Philosophy*, p. 490.

274. A. R. Wadia calls them "see-saw statements." He says they show "a conflict between the man of thought and the man of action." ("The Social Philosophy of Radhakrishnan" in *PSR*, p. 759.)

275. *A Seminar on Saints*, pp. 1-2.

276. *Counter Attack from the East*, p. 38.

277. *Radhakrishnan and Integral Experience*, p. 2.

278. "Radhakrishnan's Contribution to Universal Religion" in *PSR*, p. 369.

279. Ibid., p. 371.

280. "Radhakrishnan's Metaphysics and Ethics" in *PSR*, p. 282.

281. Ibid.

282. Ibid.

283. "Dynamic Hinduism and Radhakrishnan" in *PSR*, p. 483.

284. *Truth is Two-Eyed*, p. 103.

285. Foreword to Sarasvati Chennakesavan, *A Critical Study of Hinduism*. London: Asia Publishing House, 1974, p. vii.

286. "Radhakrishnan and the Other Vedānta" in *PSR*, pp. 462-463.

287. "Is Comparative Philosophy Possible? in *Indian Philosophy Today*, p. 211.

288. "Radhakrishnan and the Comparative Study of Religion" in *PSR*, p. 456.

289. Ibid.

290. "On Philosophical Synthesis," *Philosophy East and West*, Vol. 13, No. 2, 1963, p. 103.

291. *Humanity and Divinity*. Honolulu: University of Hawaii Press, 1970, p. x.

292. Ibid.

293. Ibid.

294. *Philosophy East and West*, Vol. 13, No. 3, 1963, p. 195.

295. Ibid., p. 196.

296. Ibid., p. 197.

297. See his *The Riddle of the World*. Third edition. Calcutta: Arya Publishing House, 1946, pp. 23-32.

298. *Introduction to Comparative Philosophy*. Carbondale: Southern Illinois University Press, 1962, p. 288.

299. Ibid.

300. Ibid., p. 291.

301. *Idealistic Thought in India*. p. 353.

302. *PSR*, p. 7.

303. See his article "Radhakrishnan in the Perspective of Indian Philosophy" in *PSR*, pp. 541-564.

304. *Radhakrishnan and Integral Experience*, p. 20.

305. *The Meeting of the East and the West in Sri Aurobindo's Philosophy*, p. 61.

306. Ibid., p. 67.

307. *Great Books of the Western World*, Vol. 1. Encyclopedia Britannica, 1959, p. 31.

308. *The Status of the Individual in East and West*. Ed. Charles A. Moore. Honolulu: University of Hawaii Press, 1968, p. 558.

309. "The Social Philosophy of Radhakrishnan" in *PSR*, p. 783.

310. Ibid.

311. Ibid., footnote 70.

312. "Radhakrishnan's Conception of the Relation between Eastern and Western Cultural Values" in *PSR*, p. 656.

313. "The Social Philosophy of Radhakrishnan" in *PSR*, p. 784.

314. One of Tagore's metaphorical descriptions of Shantiniketan was "Where the world has a nest."

315. *The Two Hands of God: The Myths of Polarity*. New York: George Braziller, 1963, p. 24.

316. *Advaita Vedānta: A Philosophical Reconstruction*, p. 14.

317. *Light, Love and Life*. Privately printed, 1987, p. 23.

318. Ibid., p. 22.

319. Troy Organ, "Polarity, A Neglected Insight in Indian Philosophy." *Philosophy East and West*, Vol. 26, No. 1, January 1976, pp. 34-35.

320. G. S. Kirk and J. E. Raven, *The Presocratic Philosophers*. Cambridge: Cambridge University Press, 1950, pp. 189, 191.

321. *The Heart of Hindusthan*, p. 40. Richard Lannoy agrees with this interpretation: "For inherent in the caste system is the acceptance of opposites without social or philosophical conflicts—unlike what would be or has been in the case in Europe." (*The Speaking Tree*, p. 168.)

322. P. 322.

323. Ibid., p. 333.

324. *PRT*, pp. 35-36.

325. Ibid., pp. 138-139.

326. Ibid., p. 152.

327. Ibid., pp. 138-139.

328. *Sādhanā*. New York: Macmillan, 1914, p. 96.

329. "Radhakrishnan's Influence on Indian Thought" in *PSR*, p. 538.

330. *The Power of Negative Thinking and Other Parables from India*. Bombay: Orient Longman, 1973, p. 124.

331. *The Speaking Tree*, pp. 173, 174.

332. *Indian Thought Through the Ages*. Bombay: Asia Publishing House, 1961, p. 174.

333. "Fragments of a Confession" in *PSR*, p. 13.

334. *The Destiny of the Mind: East and West*, p. 149.

335. *The Meeting of East and West*. New York: Macmillan, 1946, p. 447. See also "Complementary Emphases of Oriental Intuitive and Western Scientific Philosophy" in *Philosophy—East and West*. Ed. Charles A. Moore. Princeton: Princeton University Press, 1944, ch. 8; "Methodology and Epistemology, Oriental and Occidental" in *Essays in East-West Philosophy*. Ed. Charles A. Moore. Honolulu: University of Hawaii Press, 1951, ch. 7; *The Logic of the Sciences and the Humanities*. New York: Macmillan, 1947, ch. 5.

336. *Writings in Time of War*. Tr. René Hague. London: Collins, 1968, p. 178.

337. For example, *The Appearance of Man*. Tr. J. M. Cohen. London: Collins, 1965, p. 220.

338. *Writings in Time of War*, pp. 24, 78, 281.

339. *Building the Earth*. Tr. Norman Denny. London: Geoffrey-Chapmann, 1965, p. 49. Italics are Teilhard's.

340. Ibid., p. 42.

341. Introduction to *Letters from a Traveller*. Ed. Claude Aragonnès (Mlle. Teilhard-Chambon) London: Collins, 1967, p. 12.

342. Lukas and Lukas, *Teilhard*, p. 157.

343. Christopher Mooney, *Teilhard de Chardin and the Mystery of Christ*. London: Collins, 1966, p. 15.

344. Ibid., p. 13.

345. *Le Coeur de la matière*, 1950, p. 30.

346. *La Milieu Divin*. Tr. B. J. Wall et al. London: Collins, 1960, p. 95.

347. Foreword to Ursula King, *Towards a New Mysticism*. London: Collins, 1980, pp. 7, 10.

348. Ibid., p. 21.

349. *The Appearance of Man*, p. 220.

350. *The Future of Man*. Tr. Norman Denny. London: Collins, 1969, p. 316.

351. *Evolution. The Theory of Teilhard de Chardin*. London: Collins, 1969, p. 94.

352. *Christianity and Evolution*. Tr. René Hague. London: Collins, 1971, p. 132.

353. *Lettres Familières de Pierre de Chardin Mon Ami 1948-1955*. Paris, 1976, p. 225.

354. *The Phenomenon of Man*, p. 243.

355. Inaugural Address given May 29, 1955 before the Union for the Study of the Great Religions (India Branch). *Occasional Speeches and Writings. October 1952-January 1956*, p. 233.

356. *The Phenomenon of Man*, p. 27.

357. *The Future of Man*, pp. 150-151.

358. *Building the Earth*, p. 43.

359. Lukas and Lukas, *Teilhard*, p. 311.

360. *Letters of a Traveller 1923-1955*, p. 15. See also his essay "The Religious Value of Research" in *Science and Christ*. Tr. René Hague. London: Collins, 1965, pp. 199-205.

361. *Science and Christ*, p. 214.

362. Ibid., p. 217.

363. *Building the Earth*, p. 56.

364. *The Phenomenon of Man*, p. 319.

365. Ibid., pp. 319-320. Italics are Teilhard's.

366. *The Phenomenon of Man*, p. 338. See also his essay "Pantheism and Christianity" in *Christianity and Evolution*, pp. 56-75.

367. *The One and the Many*. London: Burns and Oates, 1967, p. 154.

368. *Christianity and Evolution*, p. 240.

369. Ibid., p. 34.

370. Ibid., p. 181.

371. Ibid.

372. Ibid., p. 243.

373. Ibid., pp. 143-144. Italics are Teilhard's.

374. Ibid., p. 144.

375. See *Oecuménisme* (1946), *Oeuvres* IX, pp. 253-254.

376. See *The Phenomenon of Man*, pp. 319-327.

377. For example, R. C. Zaehner, *Evolution in Religion. A Study of Sri Aurobindo and Pierre Teilhard de Chardin*. London: Oxford University Press, 1971; Jan Feys, *The Philosophy of Evolution of Sri Aurobindo and Teilhard de Chardin*. Calcutta: Firma K. L. Mukhopadhyaya, 1973; Beatrice Bruteau, *Evolution Towards Divinity*. Wheaton, Illinois: Theosophical Publication House, 1974; J. Chetany, *The Future of Man according to Teilhard de Chardin and Aurobindo Ghose*. New Delhi: Oriental Publishers, 1978.

378. "Aurobindo Ghose and Pierre Teilhard de Chardin" in *Convergence*. Ed. Paul Maroky. Vadavathoor, Kerala, India, 1981, p. 99.

379. See King, *Towards a New Mysticism*, p. 97.

380. *The Life Divine*. Sri Aurobindo Birth Centenary Library, Vol. 18. Pondicherry: Sri Aurobindo Ashram, 1970, p. 97. He also referred to an "essential and infinite Oneness which can contain the hundred and the thousand and the million and billion and trillion" (Ibid., p. 325), and to "the inevitability of the unification of the life of humanity as the result of . . . imperative natural forces." (*Sri Aurobindo Birth Centenary Library*, Vol. 27. Pondicherry: Sri Aurobindo Ashram, 1972, p. 348.)

381. *The Hindu View of Life*, p. 63.

382. *An Idealist View of Life*, p. 308.

383. "The Spirit in Man" in *Contemporary Indian Philosophy*, p. 285.

384. "Reply to Critics" in *PSR*, p. 805.

385. *An Idealist View of Life*, p. 332.

386. Ibid.

387. Ibid., p. 307.

388. Ibid.

389. Ibid.

390. Ibid.

391. *PRT*, p. 33.

392. *Eastern Religions and Western Thought*, p. 37.

393. Ibid., p. 38.

394. *An Idealist View of Life*, p. 274.

395. *Eastern Religions and Western Thought*, pp. 18-19.

396. Ibid., p. 57.

397. "Fragments of a Confession" in *PSR*, p. 30.

398. "How I Believe" in *Chrisitianity and Evolution*, p. 96. See also *Science and Christ*, pp. 14-20, 53-66.

399. "Metaphysics and Ethics in East and West" in *Essays in East-West Philosophy*, p. 421.

400. Ṛg Veda 10. 191. 4.

Recommended Readings in Comparative Philosophy

Arapura, J. G., *Radhakrishnan and Integral Experience.* (London: Asia Publishing House, 1966): 1-59.

Bahm, Archie J., *Comparative Philosophy.* (New Delhi: Vikas Publishing House, 1977.)

Bhattacharyya, K. C., "Swaraj in Ideas." *Visvabharati Quarterly*, Vol. 25, Nos. 3 and 4 (1960): 294-303.

Burtt, Edwin A., "My Path to Philosophy." *Philosophy East and West*, Vol. 22, No. 4 (1972): 429-440.

_____, "The Problem of a World Philosophy" in *Radhakrishnan. Comparative Studies in Philosophy Presented in Honour of his Sixtieth Birthday.* (London: George Allen and Unwin, 1951): 29-42.

_____, "Basic Problems of Method in Harmonizing Eastern and Western Philosophy" in *Essays in East-West Philosophy.* Ed. Charles A. Moore. (Honolulu: University of Hawaii Press, 1951): 103-123.

Chan, W. T., "The Unity of East and West" in *Radhakrishnan. Comparative Studies in Philosophy Presented in Honour of his Sixtieth Birthday.* (London: George Allen and Unwin, 1951): 104-117.

Conger, George R., "Integration" in *Essays in East-West Philosophy.* Ed. Charles A. Moore. (Honolulu: University of Hawaii Press, 1951): 271-287.

Corbin, Henry, *The Concept of Comparative Philosophy.* Tr. Peter Russell. (Ipswich: Golgonooza Press, 1981.)

Datta, Dhirendra Mohan, "On Philosophical Synthesis." *Philosophy East and West*, Vol. 13, No. 3 (1963): 195-200.

Dennes, William Ray, "Empirico-Naturalism and World Understanding" in *Essays in East-West Philosophy.* Ed. Charles A. Moore. (Honolulu: University of Hawaii Press, 1951): 124-150.

Devaraja, N. K., "Philosophy and Comparative Philosophy." *Philosophy East and West*, Vol. 17, Nos. 1-4 (1967): 51-59.

Eaton, Gail, *The Richest Vein.* (London: Faber and Faber, 1949): 9-120.

Feys, Jan, *The Philosophy of Evolution of Sri Aurobindo and Teilhard de Chardin.* (Calcutta: Firma K. L. Mukhapadh-yaya, 1973): 2-19.

Guénon, René, *East and West.* (London: Luzac, 1941): 9-19, 133-257.

_____, *Introduction to the Study of the Hindu Scriptures.* Tr. Marco Pallis. (London: Luzac, 1945): 27-69, 334-351.

Haas, William S., *The Destiny of the Mind: East and West.* (London: Faber and Faber, 1956.)

Heimann, Betty, *Indian and Western Philosophy.* (London: George Allen and Unwin, 1937.)

Hocking, William Ernest, *Living Religions and a World Faith.* (London: George Allen and Unwin, 1940):143-208.

_____, "Value of the Comparative Study of Philosophy" in *Philosophy—East and West.* Ed. Charles A. Moore. (Princeton: Princeton University Press, 1946): 1-11.

Joad, C. E. M., *Counter Attack from the East.* (London: George Allen and Unwin, 1933): 9-14, 247-264.

King, Ursula, *Towards a New Humanism.* (London: Collins, 1980): 105-218.

Leibniz, G. W. F., "On Philosophical Synthesis." Selected by Philip P. Wiener. *Philosophy East and West,* Vol. 12, No. 3 (1962): 195-202.

McCarthy, Harold E., "The Problem of Philosophical Divers-ity." *Philosophy East and West,* Vol. 9, Nos. 3 and 4 (1960): 107-128.

Malkani, G. R., "On Philosophical Synthesis." *Philosophy East and West,* Vol. 13, No. 2 (1963): 99-103.

Maroky, Paul, (Ed.), *Convergence.* (Vadavathoor, Kerala, India: Oriental Institute of Religious Studies, 1981): 3-31.

Masson-Oursel, P., *Comparative Philosophy.* (New York: Harcourt Brace, 1926): 31-69, 151-171.

Moore, Charles A., "An Attempt at World Philosophical Synthesis" in *Essays in East-West Philosophy.* Ed. Charles A. Moore. (Honolulu: University of Hawaii Press, 1951): 1-14.

_____, "Metaphysics and Ethics in East and West" in *Essays in East-West Philosophy.* Ed. Charles A. Moore. (Honolulu: University of Hawaii Press, 1951): 398-424.

Muntz, Peter, "India and the West: A Synthesis." *Philosophy East and West,* Vol. 5, No. 4 (1956): 321-338.

Nair, Seyyed Houssein, "Conditions for Meaningful Comparative Philosophy." *Philosophy East and West,* Vol. 22, No. 1 (1972): 53-61.

Nakamura, Hajime, *Parallel Developments. A Comparative History of Ideas.* (Tokyo and New York: Kodansha, 1975.)

Northrop, F.S.C., *The Meeting of East and West*. (New York: Macmillan, 1946.)

_____, "The Relation Between Eastern and Western Philosophy" in *Radhakrishnan. Comparative Studies in Philosophy Presented in Honour of his Sixtieth Birthday*. (London: George Allen and Unwin, 1951): 362-378.

Parsons, Howard L., "The Meeting of East and West in Philosophical Thought." *The Philosophical Quarterly*, (July 1958): 73-94.

Raju, P. T., "The Western and Indian Philosophical Traditions." *The Philosophical Review*, Vol. 61 (March 1927): 127-155.

_____, *An Introduction to Comparative Philosophy* (Lincoln, Nebraska: University of Nebraska Press, 1962): 251-325

Raman, N. S. S., "Is Comparative Philosophy Possible?" in *Indian Philosophy Today*. Ed. N. K. Devaraja. (Delhi: Macmillan Co. of India, 1975): 201-217.

Rao, P. Kodanda, *East Versus West. A Denial of Contrast*. (London: George Allen and Unwin, 1939.)

Rośan, Laurence J., "A Key to Comparative Philosophy." *Philosophy East and West*, Vol. 2, No. 1 (1952): 56-65, 76-78.

Saher, P. J., *Eastern Wisdom and Western Thought*. (London: George Allen and Unwin, 1969): 199-285.

Scharfstein, Ben-Ami et al., *Philosophy East/Philosophy West*. (Oxford: Basil Blackwell, 1978.)

Sheldon, Wilmon Henry, "Main Contrasts between Eastern and Western Philosophy" in *Essays in East-West Philosophy*. Ed. Charles A. Moore. (Honolulu: University of Hawaii Press, 1951): 288-297.

Ward, Barbara, *The Interplay of East and West*. (London: George Allen and Unwin, 1957.)

Watts, Alan W., *The Two Hands of God: The Myths of Polarity*. (New York: George Braziller, 1963.)

Wu, Joseph S., "Contemporary Western Philosophy from an Eastern Viewpoint." *International Philosophical Quarterly*, Vol. 8, No. 4 (December 1968): 491-497.

A Note about the Author

Troy Wilson Organ is Distinguished Professor of Philosophy Emeritus at Ohio University. The recipient of several Ford Foundation and Fulbright Research Grants, he has studied extensively in India. Among his numerous publications are *The Hindu Quest for the Perfection of Man*, *Third Eye Philosophy*, and *Western Approaches to Eastern Philosophy* (Ohio).